KICKING THE FOOTBALL

Bill Renner, MA

Head Football Coach, Langley High School
Director, 4th Down Sports Kicking Camps

Human Kinetics

Library of Congress Cataloging-in-Publication Data

Renner, Bill.
    Kicking the football / Bill Renner.
        p.   cm.
    Includes index.
    ISBN 0-88011-685-4
    1. Kicking (Football)   I. Title.
    GV951.7.R467   1997   97-12108
                                                             CIP

ISBN: 0-88011-685-4

Table 7.1 and the drills in chapters 3 and 6 previously appeared in *Complete Manual to Punting and Kicking for Players and Coaches* published by Gridiron Press in 1993.

Acquisitions Editor: Kenneth Mange; **Developmental Editor:** Kristine Enderle; **Assistant Editors:** Coree Schutter and Tony Callihan; **Editorial Assistant:** Laura Ward Majersky; **Copyeditor:** Barbara Field; **Proofreader:** Erin Cler; **Indexer:** Joan Griffitts; **Graphic Designer:** Robert Reuther; **Graphic Artist:** Denise Lowry; **Photo Editor:** Boyd LaFoon; **Cover Designer:** Jack Davis; **Photographer (cover):** Anthony Neste; **Photographer (interior):** Charles Tack, unless otherwise indicated; **Illustrators:** Paul To and Craig Ronto; **Printer:** Versa Press

Human Kinetics books are available at special discounts for bulk purchase. Special editions or book excerpts can also be created to specification. For details, contact the Special Sales Manager at Human Kinetics.

Printed in the United States of America   10   9   8   7   6   5   4   3   2

Human Kinetics
Web site: http://www.humankinetics.com/

United States: Human Kinetics, P.O. Box 5076, Champaign, IL 61825-5076
1-800-747-4457
e-mail: humank@hkusa.com

Canada: Human Kinetics, 475 Devonshire Road, Unit 100, Windsor, ON N8Y 2L5
1-800-465-7301 (in Canada only)
e-mail: humank@hkcanada.com

Europe: Human Kinetics, P.O. Box IW14, Leeds LS16 6TR, United Kingdom
+44 (0)113-278 1708
e-mail: humank@hkeurope.com

Australia: Human Kinetics, 57A Price Avenue, Lower Mitcham, South Australia 5062
(08) 82771555
e-mail: humank@hkaustralia.com

New Zealand: Human Kinetics, P.O. Box 105-231, Auckland Central
09-523-3462
e-mail: humank@hknewz.com

This book is dedicated to my mother and father. My mother, an English teacher, instilled in me my love for English and writing. My father, a career Marine and college hockey player, gave me his leadership ability and athletic ability, which enabled me to excel as an athlete and become a coach.

CONTENTS

FOREWORD

Through my playing and coaching careers, football has become a highly specialized sport. Player substitutions are based on down, distance, field position, time on the clock, play selection, match-ups, and a variety of other contingencies. Today, the two-way player is the exception, and at higher levels of play, positions are increasingly specialized. Two player positions for whom there are no substitutes are a quality placekicker and a proven punter. Their roles are unique and critical to a team's success.

At Texas, our kicking game provides the field position and point production we need to win consistently. Our kickers work hard to refine their technique and improve their performance, but we rely on athletes who have learned solid fundamentals before coming to our team. Just as there is no substitute for the proven placekicker or punter, for players who want to fill those shoes, there is no substitute for expert instruction and practice with the best technique.

Kicking the Football is for players who want to excel as placekickers and punters. It's also for coaches who want a solid kicking game. Former NFL punter Bill Renner is one of the finest kicking instructors in the world. Bill teaches all of the essential techniques, describes all of the drills, and presents the key practice pointers to correct errors and improve in each session.

This is the best single book you can use to develop the distance, accuracy, hang time, and consistency it takes to kick at a high competitive level. When a game hinges on a kickoff, field goal, or punt next season, you'll be glad you were prepared.

John Mackovic
Head Football Coach, University of Texas

PREFACE

fter five concussions (three occurring in a six-month span), I was disqualified from playing any contact football positions. I was never a star as a tailback, slotback, tight end, or defensive end, but I could always execute what the coaches wanted and do it effectively enough to contribute to the team. I could make plays because I was disciplined and motivated to do things the right way and believed that, when counted on, I could always perform.

However, my career was not over; I had another athletic challenge to conquer. I was slated to be the starting punter the next two years and had always wanted to see how good I could be at punting if I did it full time. I had never practiced only punting in college. Playing other positions in football and participating in other sports prepared me for the challenges of being solely a punter.

So I went to my first practice as a punter only. When team stretching ended, we went to the "specialists" field, and I was ready to be told what drills to do, how many footballs to punt, when to get ready for special team time, and in general, how to practice to be a successful punter. However, there were no drills. There was no coach. I had no formula for success.

I was now my own coach. It was up to me to be ready to punt, and punt well, when the head coach called on me. How I got ready to punt was my problem. This was a difficult situation for me to accept. How could I know whether what I was practicing was right or wrong? I had never been in this situation before as an athlete.

Thus began my study of how to punt and kick a football. I began to learn how to train myself physically, mentally, and technically to become a good punter. As a physical education major, my classes were tailored perfectly for me to learn how the body functions and how to train it to function more efficiently to perform to its maximum potential. I then decided to get a master's degree in exercise physiology to further my physical training knowledge. I even chose to do my master's thesis on punting.

Doing the research for my thesis also spurred me to become more conscious of the proper techniques of punting and kicking. I found there were theories but no absolute coaching techniques, drills, phrases, and so on, for teaching the skills of punting and kicking. Were the skills of punting and kicking so different they could not be coached and taught like the other football positions?

Opinions on teaching the skills fell into two categories: (1) those of coaches and players who professed to have techniques they felt worked for them to punt and kick well but may or may not work for others, or (2) those of coaches who openly admitted that they had no idea what to teach or how to perform the skills. Thus, *Kicking the Football* was written to provide you with the precise techniques and teaching sequence to learn soccer-style kicking and punting. This book details *what* to do, *how* to do it, and *why* to do it. Additionally, drills are presented for teaching each specific technique in the kicking and punting sequence.

The ability to teach or perform the skills of punting and kicking requires no unique traits. Anyone who can coach and teach any type of skill can teach punting and kicking if they understand the techniques and the teaching sequence. Anyone who has a desire to kick or punt can do so if they learn the techniques and follow a developmental plan. As you read this book, I believe you will find it an invaluable source for understanding how to teach and perform the skills.

I have always believed in a saying of legendary basketball coach John Wooden: "It is what you learn after you know it all that counts." The pursuit of learning exactly how to teach, coach, and perform the skills of punting and kicking will be endless. Hopefully, I have given you a place to begin.

Bill Renner

ACKNOWLEDGMENTS

I would like to first acknowledge all the young athletes who came through the kicking camps over the years to allow us to refine our thoughts and teaching techniques with regard to kicking and punting. In addition, a sincere thanks to all the football coaches who first asked me for advice on working with their kickers and punters and then encouraged me to put it in print.

The soccer-style kicking information in this book draws heavily from the expertise of Tom Taricani. Tom is the director of soccer-style kicking for the nationally recognized 4th Down Sports Kicking Camps. Through years of directing kicking camps together, Tom and I have developed a teaching methodology that combines his philosophy and techniques in a format consistent with my punting instruction. Tom is the real soccer-style expert, and the proven teaching model presented here is the result of our work together.

The staff at Human Kinetics and specifically, Ken Mange, and Kristine Enderle, need acknowledgment for directing this project to its completion. They have my utmost respect for their dedication, commitment, and professionalism. Their task of overseeing the transformation of my words and figures into a concise book was outstanding and they were extremely pleasurable to work with.

A most special appreciation and thank you goes to my family—Cindy, my wife; Summer, my daughter; and Bryn, my son—for their understanding and patience as I juggled the role of coach, teacher, speaker, writer, and father to complete this book. Their friendship and caring are the driving aspect of my work. In addition, many special thanks must be made to Ken and Sue Dobson. Their unconditional support, love, and encouragement have been extended to me in numerous and indescribable ways. They have made me feel more like a son than a son-in-law.

Most of all I would like to thank God for His many blessings, but specifically for giving me the ability and opportunity to have been an athlete and to coach and teach athletes.

chapter 1

PLACEKICKING TECHNIQUES

Learning what to do is important, but planning for your development is the mechanism that develops your ability. Know what part of the kick you should develop first and place emphasis on mastering it. The measuring stick you will be judged by is how many field goals you can make—your accuracy. Everything you do should relate to making you better in that regard. This must be your developmental philosophy in planning what part of the kick you will work on daily or weekly.

Sequencing your kicking development in the proper order ensures you are working on the mechanics that will have the greatest performance impact. Focusing on kicking factors that do not develop accuracy, height, or distance is a waste of practice time. Start with the skills that affect accuracy and progress to those that develop distance.

The sequence begins with development of foot-to-ball contact and progresses to situation kicking. Some level of mastery of each phase is necessary before moving to the next phase. It is difficult to learn more than one technique at a time and still be effective in changing a technique. Don't be in a hurry to move forward to the next developmental level until you have achieved some degree of mastery at the current level.

Set a performance goal for each level and hold yourself accountable for achieving it as a measure of your mastery of that skill. For example, a mastery-level goal for the foot-to-ball contact phase might be to contact 10 footballs perfectly so that you hit the ball in the sweet spot with the right part of your foot and the ball rotates the right way. Test yourself daily or every other day at the end of your drills, and when you have reached this goal, shift the majority of your practice time to a new phase.

KICKING INSTRUCTIONAL SEQUENCE
Foot-to-Ball Contact
Leg Swing Techniques
Approach Steps
Stance
Kickoffs
Situation Kicking

Develop some type of plan for learning the entire kicking skill and proceed with it until you have obtained a comfortable level of performance. An old axiom states that "if you fail to plan, then plan to fail." Leave nothing to chance with regard to your technique development and you can become the type of kicker you want to be. Good kickers are well-trained and disciplined in techniques because they practice the right things the right way. Anyone can do it. Make a plan, and then commit to follow it.

Your first step in becoming a successful placekicker is to analyze how you kick by breaking down your technique into the key components of placekicking: alignment, stance, approach, rotation and foot plant, leg swing, contact, and finishing movement. An explanation of placekicking techniques will increase your understanding and allow you to perfect your talents and become a skillful kicker.

This book begins with the kicker standing at the football to take his alignment steps and continues through the entire kick, finishing with the follow-through body position. Topics such as approach distance, lateral distance, stance, approach steps, rotational energy, plant foot position, body movement during the leg swing, the proper leg swing, contacting the football, finishing the kick, and many others are described in detail.

ALIGNMENT STEPS

No phase is more important to your success as a placekicker than aligning to kick the football. Starting at the precise spot that will place you in the optimum kicking position is the desired objective. Numerous factors can cause you to vary your starting spot when you use only *steps* to determine its location. Going backward at varying angles from the football or taking shorter or longer steps are two examples of potential stepping mistakes.

Use distance (yards) as a measure to determine exactly how to align yourself to kick the football. To find your starting spot, you need two distance measures: an approach distance and a lateral distance. Steps will be the method and yards will be the measurement tool to place you at the correct starting position.

Determining Your Starting Spot

The starting spot can vary with each individual. Variables such as leg length and kicking approach angle influence the optimum starting spot. Therefore, it is important to identify your own starting spot through trial and error. To determine your optimal starting spot, follow these general guidelines.

Stand directly behind the football so that your body, hips, shoulders, feet, the football, and the goalposts are in a straight line. Place your kicking foot directly behind and approximately four inches from the back of the football. Place your plant or nonkicking foot in the exact position you want it to be when it is planted, generally 8 to 10 inches or a shoe length to the side of the football (figure 1.1). The depth of your plant foot behind the football will vary depending on whether you are kicking off a two-inch tee, a one-inch tee, or the ground.

Figure 1.1 Placement of nonkicking foot prior to approach steps.

When kicking off a two-inch tee, position your plant or nonkicking foot with the toes one to two inches behind the *back end* of the tee. When using a one-inch tee, your plant foot is positioned with the toes even with the *back end* of the tee. When kicking off the ground, the toes of your plant foot are across from the *middle* of the football. Your plant foot should also be in these positions when you execute your kick.

Stepping Off the Starting Spot

Once you have assumed the proper plant foot placement, begin with your plant foot and take three steps backward, stop, and check your alignment to the goalposts again. Be sure that when stepping backward, you did not move at an angle to the left or right (figure 1.2). At this point, you should also pause to visualize the kick traveling through the goalposts. This mental imagery is important to foster positive thinking and give you confidence in your kick just prior to performing.

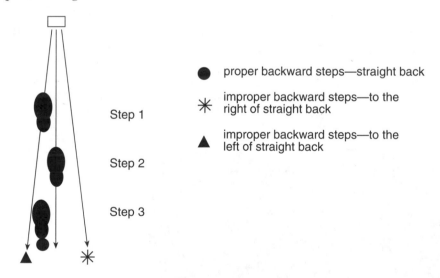

Figure 1.2 Aligning to begin the approach steps.

Use your kicking foot, the football, and the middle of the goalposts to align yourself with your target. At this point, all three should be in a straight line and you should be approximately three yards behind the football. It does not matter whether you use three or four steps to get to this spot. However, if you are more than three yards behind the ball when you reach this position, either take three steps back instead of four or take shorter strides when using four steps.

Importance of the Approach Distance. Three yards back from the football is the appropriate depth to generate the kinetic (moving) energy needed to produce distance on the kick without increasing the time to get to the ball. Standing any farther back will require you to hurry your approach to the football, affecting your swing rhythm and that of the hold-to-kick sequence.

Standing less than the three yards back reduces the amount of kinetic energy you can build to transfer to the kick. Kickers who possess greater muscular strength than others can use a shorter approach and still generate adequate distance on their kicks; however, beginning with a three-yard approach will help you maximize your physical ability.

Lateral Distance. The lateral distance is the distance you move sideways from the approach distance spot. The lateral distance affects the angle of the path you take to kick the football. The farther to the side you align yourself, the wider, more circular path you take when approaching the football (figure 1.3). The shorter the lateral distance, the more linear your approach to the football will be (figure 1.4).

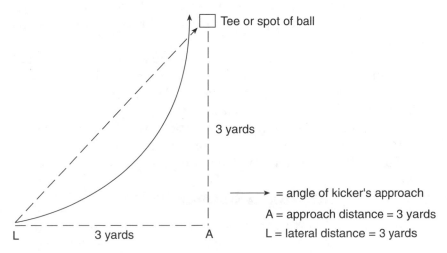

☐ Tee or spot of ball

3 yards

⟶ = angle of kicker's approach

A = approach distance = 3 yards

L = lateral distance = 3 yards

L   3 yards   A

Figure 1.3 Wider, more circular path to the kick.

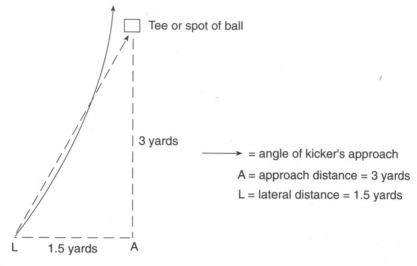

Figure 1.4 Narrower, more linear path to the kick.

Your approach path to the football will always be somewhat circular. This circular path adds rotational energy to the swing, which is why soccer-style kicking advocates believe a soccer-style kicker can kick a football farther than a straight-on kicker. However, using rotational energy for more power requires you to become proficient at rotating your body to the same spot every time you kick the football. If you do not, the distance and direction of your kicks will be inconsistent.

Generally, the wider the lateral path you take, the more rotational energy you generate, but the harder it is to rotate consistently to the proper kicking position. You will have good distance and power but will be unable to control the direction of your kicks. Using a narrow lateral path will enable you to rotate consistently to the proper spot but with potentially less power. As a result, you may be an accurate kicker but will lack distance or power on your kicks.

Determining the Proper Lateral Distance

Choosing a lateral starting distance is more a matter of individual preference than strict rule. Generally, you should align between 1.5 and 2 yards sideways from the football (figure 1.5). This distance

Figure 1.5 Lateral starting distance.

gives you a proper complement of rotational and linear movement to the football and enables you to rotate to the same spot easily.

To reach this spot from the approach distance spot, begin with your nonkicking foot and take two lateral steps, keeping your shoulders and hips facing square to the goalposts. Stop at this point and check the actual distance covered by your steps to avoid inadvertent inconsistency in steps, as previously mentioned. You may take two or three steps to reach your lateral starting point as long as you are 1.5 to 2 yards to the side.

Placing marks at the approach distance behind the tee (3 yards) and the lateral distance (1.5 to 2 yards) you need to step off consistently is an excellent teaching tool (figure 1.6). These marks keep your alignment steps consistent and train your body to know exactly what it feels like to make these steps. By practicing with the markings, your muscles will memorize the movements and enable you to align yourself on the field in exactly the same position as if the markings were there.

Figure 1.6 Marking approach and lateral starting points for instruction.

Alignment Procedures

❑ Stand directly behind the football with your hips, shoulders, feet, the football, and the goalposts in a straight line.

❑ Place your plant foot in the exact position for kicking the football, with your kicking foot comfortably positioned four inches behind the ball.

❑ Take three steps backward, stop, and check your alignment for going straight backward with the goalposts and the football. This is your *approach distance.*

❑ Visualize your kick traveling through the uprights.

❑ Move 1.5 to 2 yards laterally, keeping your shoulders and hips facing square to the goalposts. This is your *lateral distance.*

THE SOCCER-STYLE KICKER'S STANCE

A balanced, comfortable stance allows you to start your movement forward to the ball with no wasted movement. As the statement "all good things have a good beginning" implies, the stance coordinates the upper body balance and weight transfer in the hips. An unbalanced stance requires you to make adjustments during the approach or swing phase to get in the proper body position.

The correct position is the *athletic position*. To be in athletic position, your shoulders must be directly over your knees and your knees directly over your toes. This stance keeps your body balanced around its center of gravity and permits quick, efficient movement in all directions. It is the same stance football coaches teach linebackers, defensive backs, quarterbacks, and tailbacks. It is the same position a tennis player uses when receiving serve, a base runner when taking a lead, or a hockey goalie when defending the goal.

Finding Your Stance

Stand with your kicking foot about two to four inches behind your nonkicking foot in a comfortable relationship (figure 1.7). The forward or nonkicking foot should point directly at the front of the tee. This will ensure that your hips and shoulders are in the same position each time, promoting consistent hip rotation and putting you on the same approach path to the football.

Figure 1.7 Kicker's foot positions in the stance.

Taking different approach paths to the football puts you in different positions to kick the ball. Consistency in making the approach path to the football is a key element in becoming a consistent ball striker and getting to your optimum kicking position.

In the proper stance, your body is bent slightly at the knees and hips, placing the knee of your nonkicking leg slightly over your toes (figure 1.8). Your shoulders are also leaning slightly forward over your knees. This is the kicker's version of the athletic position.

Figure 1.8 Kicker's stance.

Distributing Your Weight

Distribute your weight primarily on the ball and toes of your nonkicking foot. Keep your head down and your eyes focused on the spot where the ball will be placed as you wait for the center to snap the football. To emphasize this, think of keeping your face on the football until you hit it. If your face stays down and you look at the football on ball contact, your shoulders will stay forward and your body will remain in the athletic position. This is advantageous for a powerful kick.

Aligning in a proper stance gives you a good beginning to make your kick. A bad stance can disrupt the rhythm and timing of your approach to the football and force a bad swing.

Stance Technique

❏ Stand with your kicking foot two to four inches behind your nonkicking foot in a comfortable relationship.

❏ Point the toe of your forward (nonkicking) foot at the front of the tee.

❏ Bend slightly at the knees so that your knees are over your toes.

❏ Lean forward at the waist and hips so that your shoulders are over your knees.

❏ Distribute the weight of your body on the ball and toes of the forward (nonkicking) foot.

❏ Let your head lean downward with the lean of your shoulders.

❏ Keep your eyes on the spot where the football will be placed.

APPROACH STEPS FOR A SOCCER-STYLE KICK

Besides your kicking leg strength, your approach steps to the football are the element of the kick that allows you to kick the football far. If your approach steps added nothing to the kick, it would be best to kick with one approach step or to take minimal approach steps. This is because the fewer approach steps you take, the more accurate you can be in placing your plant foot in the proper position. Keeping your momentum (weight) forward and your approach steps aimed directly at the football will enable maximum transfer of kinetic energy to the football on contact.

Finding the Proper Approach Path

A proper approach path is one that has an aiming point, maintains an inside track to the football, and has a consistent stepping pattern. Failure to be consistent in these three areas produces errors in plant foot placement and leg swing, causing inconsistency in the height, distance, and direction of your kicks.

Your plant foot aiming point directs your approach path steps to the football. Your approach path aiming point is the front end of the tee when kicking off a tee (figure 1.9). When kicking off the ground, your aiming point is a spot four inches in front of where the football will be placed (figure 1.10). Your nonkicking toe should be pointing at these landmarks when you have assumed your stance.

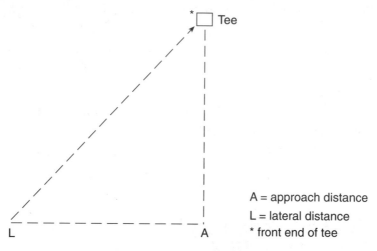

Figure 1.9 Approach path aiming point using a tee.

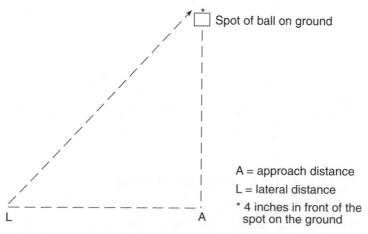

Figure 1.10 Approach path aiming point kicking off the ground.

The proper approach path is one that keeps you on an inside track to the football so that your leg swing starts inside, squares to the football, and finishes inside as you follow through (figure 1.11).

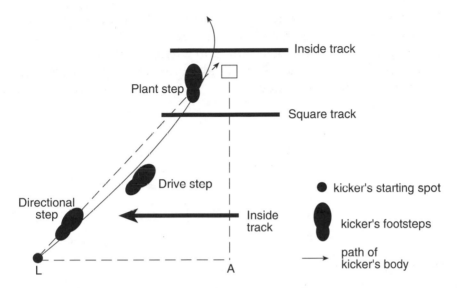

Figure 1.11 Kicker's inside-square-inside approach path.

An approach path that takes you to the right of or toward the back of the football will cause you to overrotate and plant your foot with the toe pointing to the left of your target. This is caused by aligning with your foot pointing behind the tee, resulting in contacting the football too late in the leg swing. As a result, your kicks will travel to the left of your target.

An approach path that takes you too far to the left of the correct approach path results in your plant foot toe pointing to the right of your target. This is caused by aligning with your foot pointing too far in front of the tee, resulting in contacting the football too early in the leg swing. As a result, your kicks will travel to the right of your target.

Directional Step. To begin your approach steps, simply fall forward, leading with your shoulders. This will cause you to take a short six- to eight-inch directional step with your nonkicking leg. This directional step sets the approach path you take to kick the football. This is extremely important because it ultimately determines the depth of your plant foot in relation to the football. A poor plant foot position results in a mis-hit kick or a loss of maximum height or distance on your kick. Periodically check the direction of your first step to ensure you have the proper approach path to the football.

To practice this technique, draw a line with marking paint from the toe of your nonkicking foot when you are in your stance to the front end of the tee or football, depending on whether you are using a tee (figure 1.12). Even experienced kickers should do this periodically to monitor their directional step.

Figure 1.12   Marking the approach path for training.

If your directional step is inside the approach path, your body will rotate more than you aligned yourself for. When your directional step is outside the approach path, your body will rotate less. In either case, a bad directional step has resulted in a different rotation. The result will be differences in the height, distance, and accuracy of your kicks.

Drive Step.   The second step, called the drive step, is a little longer than a normal stride length. The actual distance of this step varies with the height and leg length of the kicker. When your foot has contacted the ground in the drive-step position, your toe and knee are pointing toward the football and your body weight is on the ball and toes of your drive-step foot, extending down the inside of the arch. Drive or push hard off this step to accelerate your body to the plant step (figure 1.13).

When in the drive-step position, your upper and lower body are rotated to the right of the target or goalposts. Your degree of rotation

Figure 1.13 Body position during the drive step.

away from the target is preset by the alignment of your shoulders and hips in the stance. It remains constant as you take your first step in the proper direction, establishing the correct approach path to the football.

Remember, to have command of any skill, your techniques *must* be consistent. Taking the proper stance and first or directional step to kick the football has a tremendous impact on positioning of the drive step and ultimately on the success of your kick.

Soccer-Style Kick Approach Technique

❏ Aim the toe of your forward (nonkicking) foot directly at the front end of the tee. This is your *approach path.*

❏ Take a short six- to eight-inch step toward the football by leaning forward from your shoulders. This is your *directional step.*

❏ Take a second step toward the football with your kicking foot. This is your *drive step.*

❏ When your drive foot is planted, your toe and knee are turned outward, pointing at the football, and your upper and lower body are rotated to the right of the target.

ROTATION AND PLANT FOOT PLACEMENT

Rotational energy is the theoretical advantage a soccer-style kicker has over a straight-on kicker. Rotational energy can have a negative or positive impact on the soccer-style kick. To develop some degree of mastery over the flight of the football, you must first develop the ability to rotate your body so that your shoulders, hips, and plant toe are pointing directly at your target on impact.

Rotating to the Plant Position

Regardless of the techniques used prior to planting the foot to kick the football, every kicker must be *square* to the target on impact with the ball to ensure it will go straight toward the target. A square position is having the toe and knee of your plant foot and your hips, shoulders, and body pointing directly at the target. If these areas are aligned with and pointing to the target, you can control the direction of the kick with your leg swing.

Squaring up to your target is a trainable technique. Improving your ability to get to the square position repeatedly is the first step in improving your accuracy. As a kicker, accuracy is the best trait you can possess. The *most accurate* kickers are those who can rotate to the square position more often and more precisely than others. The *best* kickers are those who can do it in the face of adversity.

Placing Your Plant Foot

The plant foot is the axis point for the leg swing. Where it is placed in relation to the lateral distance to the football and behind or next to the ball determines whether the ball is contacted on the ascending or descending part of the leg swing and whether the ball is contacted in the sweet spot.

The proper plant foot position is the exact same spot at which your feet are positioned to begin marking off your approach steps. As a reminder, this position changes according to whether you are kicking off a tee or the ground.

Use these generic starting points to determine your optimal plant foot position. This position may vary slightly for each kicker, depending on his leg length and natural leg swing. However, when learning or teaching the soccer-style kick, it is a good idea to begin with these landmarks.

Determining Your Plant Foot Placement and Direction

An effective way to determine your proper plant foot position is to mark this spot with field-marking paint prior to kicking. Mark a six- to eight-inch line starting a shoe length from the football to denote the (lateral) distance your plant foot should be from the football. This mark is parallel to the tee. Mark another six- to eight-inch line to denote the distance to plant your foot behind the football using a line perpendicular to the first line. The resulting mark is an "L," or a type of "batter's box" for your plant foot (figure 1.14). As you kick, the toe of your plant foot should be on or behind the horizontal stroke of the "L" and your foot should be placed to the inside of the centerline (downstroke) of the "L."

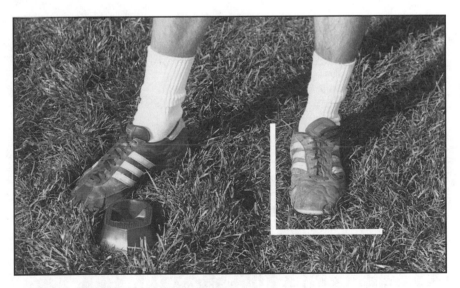

Figure 1.14 Making a box for teaching plant foot placement.

Monitor the height and distance of your kicks. If the football does not elevate as well as it should, move the "L" backward, causing the toe of your plant foot to be positioned farther behind the football. This permits contact with the football as your leg is ascending. If you move your plant foot too far back, you will notice you are contacting the ball above the sweet spot, resulting in wobbly, line-drive kicks.

By simply manipulating where the toe of your plant foot is placed relative to the depth of the football, you can control the spot where your foot hits the ball. When you can contact the sweet spot of the football consistently, note the location of the toe of your plant foot relative to the ball or tee and you have determined your optimal plant foot placement.

The direction your plant foot toe points also has an impact on your leg swing. The optimal path is an inside-square-inside track. Pointing your toe directly at the target allows your leg to swing along this track. If the toe of your plant foot points to the left of the target, your leg swing will travel on an outside-in path, and you will pull the football to the left. If the toe of your plant foot points to the right of your target, your leg swing will travel on an inside-out path, and you will push the football to the right of your target.

Rotation and Plant Foot Placement Technique

❏ Rotate the knee of your plant foot and your hips, shoulders, and body SQUARE to the goalposts.

❏ Rotate and point the toe of your plant foot directly at the middle of the goalposts.

❏ Place your plant foot one shoe length away and to the side of the football.

❏ Place your plant foot toe one to two inches behind the tee when kicking off a two-inch block, even with the back of the tee when kicking off a one-inch block, and across from the middle of the football when kicking off the ground.

LEG SWING FOR A SOCCER-STYLE KICK

A good leg swing has several noticeable characteristics. Your leg is fully flexed behind your body with your heel almost touching your buttock before beginning its descending path toward the football. Your swing is a smooth, rhythmical, attacking motion prior to contact and as it accelerates through the football. Your leg creates a long, fluid line from toe to hip when fully extended, which is noticeable at ball contact and throughout the follow-through. After contacting the football and as it is decelerating, your leg continues on a path that travels slightly across your body to your opposite shoulder.

Positioning Your Leg Swing Path

Even though the term *soccer style* is used, kicking a football requires a different leg swing than kicking a soccer ball. The leg swing used to kick a soccer ball is a flat, sweeping motion. The leg swing for kicking a football is an abrupt descending and ascending motion that facilitates lifting the football into the air. These leg swings differ because the sweet spot of a soccer ball is lower to the ground than that of a football when it is on a tee.

When viewed from the side, your leg swing path should take the shape of a parabola; that is, it should have the same slope on the descending and ascending sides of the axis (figure 1.15). The heel of your plant foot is the lowest point of your leg swing. By moving the toe of your plant foot backward or forward relative to the football, you can manipulate where your foot contacts the ball during the leg swing (figure 1.16).

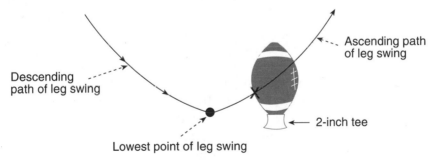

Descending path of leg swing

Ascending path of leg swing

2-inch tee

Lowest point of leg swing

● = plant foot heel

X = indicates "sweet spot" to contact the football

Figure 1.15 Leg swing path.

Leg Swing Contact Point. The football should be contacted on the ascending portion of the leg swing for two reasons. First, at some point during the ascending portion of the leg swing, your leg will be traveling at maximum speed. The exact location of the leg at maximum velocity varies slightly with each individual; generally,

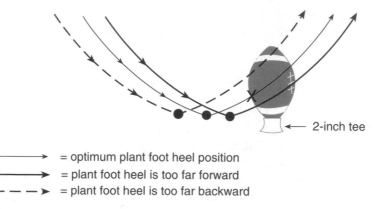

──────▶	= optimum plant foot heel position
──────▶	= plant foot heel is too far forward
─ ─ ─ ▶	= plant foot heel is too far backward

Figure 1.16 Affecting the leg swing path by moving the plant foot.

however, the foot should contact the ball after it has passed its lowest point, the heel of the nonkicking foot. This would position the foot-to-ball contact beyond the toe of the nonkicking foot.

Second, the ascending path of the leg swing assists in the lift or height the football achieves. This is because the hips generate energy as they uncoil from the flexed position during the initial phase of the leg swing ascension and transfer that energy to the collision between the foot and the ball on contact. In other words, the hips accelerate the body through the football.

The uncoiling or "roll" of the hips is the same technique taught to linemen, linebackers, and running backs. The roll of the hips for blocking, tackling, and kicking a football carries the speed of the body through the contact point of the collision and ensures maximum transfer of energy to the contacted object. If you do not accelerate your hips through the contact point, you are not using the power of your body to kick the football. You are kicking with the strength of your kicking leg only.

Contacting the football during the descending portion of your leg swing is evidenced by low, line-drive kicks that don't travel as far as normal. This leg swing looks as if you have punched at the football instead of making a fluid, rhythmical swing. Because your leg is still descending, your leg muscles have not had a chance to contract fully. This keeps your leg from reaching maximum velocity prior to contacting the football. Placing your plant foot in the correct location ensures that you will be in the proper position to uncoil your hips as you kick.

Body Movement During the Leg Swing. As your plant foot contacts the ground and you initiate your leg swing, your upper body should be leaning slightly backward. You will only be in this position momentarily. At this instant, the power of your body is leaning away from the football. To use this accumulated power, your upper body must return to the athletic position at contact and remain there throughout the follow-through of your leg swing.

To facilitate this movement, your weight is shifted from an even distribution along your plant foot to the ball and toe of that foot. This weight shift begins to return your body from leaning backward to the athletic position. As your leg follows through after contact with the football, your upper body bends at the waist so that your shoulders meet your leg as it swings slightly across your body. However, it is primarily the impetus of the leg swing that causes the leg and shoulder to come together, not the shoulders bending to meet the leg.

Dipping your shoulders to "keep your head down" causes the location of the lowest point of your leg swing to alter. It moves this point forward, causing the football to be contacted on the descending portion of your leg swing. This produces line-drive kicks or kicks that are lower than normal. Distance is also affected, because the football is not contacted when the kicking leg has contracted or reached maximum velocity.

Your Plant Foot During the Leg Swing. Begin plant foot placement by planting your heel first and then rolling onto (shifting your weight to) your toes. At this point, your plant foot will act as either an accelerator or a brake to your body's movement. The desired result is that it will act as an accelerator. As an accelerator it facilitates the roll of your hips and the transfer of your body's momentum into kicking the football. This is due to shifting your weight from your heel to your toes. During the ascension of your leg swing, your weight is evenly distributed. As your kicking foot contacts the football, 90 percent of the weight on your plant foot has shifted to the ball of your foot, and your heel begins to lift off the ground.

As your leg swing continues to ascend after contact, the heel of your plant foot comes completely off the ground and your toes push your body (plant foot accelerator) past the point where the football was contacted (figure 1.17). The push of your plant foot will propel your body off the ground, and forward 12 to 14 inches downfield.

Pushing your body past the point of ball contact is essential for maximum transfer of body energy to the football.

Figure 1.17 Pushing with the plant foot.

Pushing properly with your plant foot will leave noticeable marks as you kick. One mark can be seen where you place your plant foot to kick the football. A second mark should be detected 12 to 14 inches in front of the tee pointing directly at the target. If the second mark is pointing to the left of the target, you are falling away from the football as you kick and need to be more balanced on your plant foot.

The direction you push your plant foot affects the accuracy of your kick. Push your body straight downfield to keep the football traveling straight at its intended target. If your body falls to the left or right as you push through the contact point, the football will not travel straight. The flight of the ball will be to the left or right of the target according to the push of your plant foot.

Leg Swing Technique

❑ Fully flex your leg behind your body with the heel almost touching the buttock.

❏ Make an abrupt descending motion directly at the football to begin the leg swing.

❏ The heel of your plant foot is the lowest point of the leg swing.

❏ The leg swing should be a smooth, rhythmical, attacking pendulum motion prior to, during, and after contact with the football. It should ascend at the same abrupt angle as it descended.

❏ Contact the football on the ascending portion of the leg swing.

❏ Your leg should remain fully extended, creating a long, fluid line from toe to hip as it follows through on a path that travels slightly across your body to the opposite shoulder.

Body Movement Technique

❏ As your plant foot contacts the ground, your upper body leans slightly backward from the athletic position.

❏ Return your upper body to the athletic position as you begin the descending portion of the leg swing while shifting your weight from the heel to the ball and toes of your plant foot.

❏ Your upper body is vertical or slightly behind vertical as you contact the football.

❏ As your leg follows through, your upper body bends at the waist so your leg meets your shoulders as it swings upward on the follow-through.

Plant Foot Technique

❏ The heel of your plant foot hits the ground first as it is planted.

❏ Distribute your weight evenly on your plant foot as you flex your leg for the leg swing.

❏ Transfer your weight from an even distribution to the ball and toes of your plant foot as your leg descends to kick the football.

❏ Push forcefully and aggressively with your plant foot just after initial contact with the football.

❏ Your plant foot push will carry your body past the football, off the ground, and 12 to 14 inches forward down the field.

FOOT-TO-BALL CONTACT

The ability to contact the football consistently in the sweet spot, the spot that will provide optimal transfer of energy from your leg, body, and kicking mechanics to the football, is the skill that separates good kickers from those who are the best. All other kicking mechanics are important, but none is more important than being a good ball contactor. If you can strike the football in the proper location, you can perform some of the kicking mechanics different from the accepted standard and still be a good kicker.

The position of your foot, the position of the football, the location of the sweet spot, and the part of the foot contacting the football are the elements of good foot-to-ball contact. Performing all the kicking mechanics correctly can still produce an undesired result if the ball is not contacted properly. Adhering to and focusing on this technique are the last things that should go through your mind as you align and prepare for the kick.

Positioning the Plant Foot for Ball Contact

Placing your plant foot too far in front of or too far behind the football will result in a leg swing that does not contact the sweet spot. The depth of your plant foot determines which part of the football is contacted by the leg swing. If you plant your foot in front of the optimal plant foot position, you will contact the ball below the sweet spot. This type of ball contact produces a kick that spins fast, has good height, but lacks distance.

If you plant your foot behind the optimal plant foot position, you will contact the ball above the sweet spot. This type of ball contact produces a low, line-drive kick with minimal rotation. Being able to place your plant foot properly increases your accuracy because you increase the number of times you strike the football in the correct spot. Follow the previously discussed techniques for proper plant foot toe placement.

Foot Position. Your kicking foot should be angled so that your toe points toward the holder rather than the ground. This allows you to kick the football without your toe hitting the ground. Point your toe maximally to create a smooth, rigid surface for contact with the football. Bending your ankle even slightly prevents maximum transfer of energy from your leg to the football. This is because some of the energy in the collision between your foot and the ball will be lost when you straighten your ankle as the ball is contacted.

Rotate your kicking foot inward to expose the top of the foot to the football (figure 1.18). When your foot is rotated inward, the hip of your kicking leg also rotates, causing the top of your foot, your knee, and the hip of your kicking leg to face the target. Emphasize pointing your knee at the target to align your body square to the target automatically.

Figure 1.18 Kicking foot position for ball contact.

You want to contact the football on the large bone on top of your foot, above the arch. The approximate location is the inward side of the laces of your kicking foot shoe. This is the best place to contact the football because it is the sturdiest part of the top of your foot. Contacting the football with any other part of the foot, toes, or ankle will not produce maximum transfer of energy to the football because some of the energy will be lost in the collision between the foot and the ball.

Football Position. The football is held almost vertical, or straight up and down (figure 1.19). Leaning the ball backward about a quarter inch rotates the sweet spot downward just enough to make it easier to contact than if the ball were straight up and down. Positioning the football correctly is important because the more it is tilted backward, the lower the sweet spot will be to the ground.

Figure 1.19 Vertical ball position for the kick.

The lower the sweet spot is to the ground, the harder it is to contact. The lower the sweet spot, the more sweeping and flat your leg swing must be and the more difficult it will be to get height on the kick.

Most soccer-style kickers like the holder to pull the football about an inch toward himself. This moves the sweet spot slightly to the right for a right-footed kicker and tends to align it better to meet the large bone of the kicking foot as it swings through to contact the ball. Having the holder pull the ball toward himself promotes better contact between the foot and the ball and reduces the number of mis-hit kicks.

Tilting the football in any direction can change the location of the sweet spot. Varying the tilt of the football leads to inconsistent ball contact because it puts the sweet spot in a different location each time. The primary job of the holder is to present the football to the kicker the same way every time.

The holder cannot be expected to place the football in exactly the same location every time. Missing the placement spot by a slight margin will not affect the height, distance, or accuracy of the kick; however, the holder should be expected to tilt the football the same way every time.

Do not be distracted from concentrating on kicking mechanics and preparing mentally for the kick by focusing on the hold of the football. Average or marginal kickers tend to worry about how the ball is held, correcting how the holder does his job or blaming the holder for their own lack of execution. Take full responsibility for your kick and work on what you can control to ensure it is executed successfully.

No one wants to hear excuses for why you failed. They just want to see you execute the skill. The only way to do so consistently is to focus on what you can control, not on what is beyond your control. Unless you would rather be the holder's coach than the kicker, learn to disregard how the football is presented and develop the attitude that you can kick the football well regardless of the hold. You will learn higher level thinking and develop the confidence it takes to be an elite-level kicker.

Locating the Sweet Spot

The sweet spot is located about four inches above the tip of the football. For high school kickers, this is slightly above the white stripe. When this spot is contacted with the ascending motion of the kicking foot, maximal transfer of energy will take place, because this is where the greatest surface area of the football is located. Contacting the football above or below this spot causes its flight to lack either distance, height, or accuracy.

Contacting the Football Technique

❑ Angle your kicking foot so that your toe points toward the holder.

❑ Point your toe maximally to create a smooth, rigid surface with which to contact the football.

❑ Rotate your kicking foot inward to expose the top of your foot to the football; this will also rotate the hip of your kicking leg inward.

❏ Point the knee of your kicking leg at the target to align the foot, knee, and hip directly at the goalposts.

❏ Contact the football on the large bone on top of your foot, above the arch.

❏ Have the holder position the football so that it is leaning slightly backward a quarter inch, or almost vertical. The holder should pull the football toward himself about one inch.

❏ Contact the football about four inches above the tip end—on the *sweet spot*.

FINISHING MOVES

What your leg swing does after contact with the football does not affect the kick itself yet is significant for other reasons. Once the football has been contacted by your leg, the energy to make it fly has been transferred and it is already traveling toward its intended target. Thus, what your body does after ball contact has no effect on the height, distance, or accuracy of the kick. However, because the mechanics of the follow-through and finish of the kick have an impact on the kicking mechanics *prior* to ball contact, it is important to adhere to some minimal standards.

Focusing too much on what you look like when you finish your kick is wasted practice time. The objective is to perfect techniques that will affect either the height, distance, or accuracy of the kick. Spend 99 percent of your practice time on your mechanics prior to and during contacting of the football. Once you have developed some consistency with these techniques, you will generally see improved consistency in the finish of your kicks.

Swinging Your Leg After Ball Contact

After contacting the football, your kicking leg must swing straight through the ball for 8 to 10 inches (figure 1.20). Your leg will then begin to travel slightly across the center of your body, finishing in line with the shoulder opposite your kicking leg. This slight cross-over is natural for a soccer-style placekicker.

Figure 1.20 The kicker's straight follow-through.

Too much crossover is disadvantageous to controlling the football's direction of flight. In addition, an abrupt crossover of your leg swing after contacting the football indicates a sweeping, rotational leg swing instead of the desired descending and ascending path described previously.

There is an important contact zone in which your leg must swing straight to the football, be square to the ball at contact, and then swing straight to the target after contact. This contact zone ranges from approximately eight inches behind to eight inches in front of the football. If you can swing your foot straight through this zone, the football will travel straight.

If your swing path in this zone is from the outside right of the football across to the inside left, it will direct the ball to the left of the target. Conversely, swinging from the inside left of the football across to the outside right will direct the ball to the right of the target.

There is room for individual variance from normal leg swing techniques. Variance is acceptable on the downward path of your leg swing and on the upward path in the follow-through.

If you can swing your leg straight through the contact zone consistently, don't try to change your leg swing techniques prior to and after contact with the football. Just note any differences from the standard techniques and monitor them, along with the flight of the football, in case you lose control of the direction of your kicks.

Following Through to Finish

As stated earlier, the leg swing follow-through does not affect the height, distance, or accuracy of the kick. At this point, the football has been contacted and is on its directional path to the target. The purpose of the follow-through is to decelerate your leg from its powerful swing. A full, fluid follow-through also ensures your leg is accelerating, not decelerating, before contact with the football.

Fully extend your leg at the knee, forming a straight line from toe to hip as you follow through. Your leg should remain like this as it continues to decelerate and finish at the opposite shoulder. Your leg acts as a pendulum, making a smooth, rhythmical swing to the football, and finishes with the same smooth, rhythmical movement on the follow-through.

Do not lean sideways or away from the football because it will affect the swing path of your leg. It will result in a right-to-left leg swing and cause you to pull the football to the left of the target. If you are pushing slightly to the left with your plant leg on the follow-through and are still able to control the accuracy of the football, do not attempt to change this technique. Note it as a possible correctable technique in case you begin to have accuracy problems.

Balancing the Finish

When you complete the kick, your kicking leg should return to the ground in a controlled manner and your body should be in a balanced position. Your hips and shoulders should be square to the goalposts, and your body should be one yard in front of the tee. If you complete your kick with your body falling off to the side, you did not have a balanced, controlled leg swing (figure 1.21).

If you swing uncontrollably at the football, you will be unable to control the height, distance, or accuracy of your kicks. You will be an inconsistent ball contactor, going through stages where you will kick the football well but then appearing to "lose it" suddenly. If you finish with your body next to or only slightly in front of the tee, you are not accelerating your body into the football and may even be decelerating when the football is contacted.

Figure 1.21 A balanced finish to the kick.

It is better to have a full, fluid, aggressive, balanced swing than to swing too easily. The worst thing you can do is not kick the football far enough to get it to the goalposts and give it a chance to go through. Pushing aggressively with your plant foot ensures you are using your entire body to kick the football.

Finishing Moves Technique

❑ Keep your kicking leg traveling straight at the goalposts for 8 to 10 inches after contacting the football.

❑ Your leg swing should begin to travel across the center of your body beyond the 8- to 10-inch zone.

❑ Your leg swing should contact your chest while your head is down and your eyes are on the spot where the football was held.

❏ Your leg swing should finish with a full, fluid follow-through that decelerates slowly.

❏ Your leg swing should finish in line with the opposite shoulder.

❏ Your kicking leg should return to the ground in a controlled manner with your body in a balanced position and square to the goalposts.

❏ When you finish the kick, your body should be in front of the tee.

MAXIMUM HEIGHT AND DISTANCE

Two areas where you generate power to the football are the strength and speed of your kicking leg. The kinetic energy from taking steps to kick the football generates speed for your kicking leg. The push of your plant foot transfers that speed to the football. The strength of your kicking leg does not change significantly from kick to kick. Inadvertently varying the amount and aggressiveness of your plant foot push is the leg speed factor that varies the height and distance from kick to kick.

If the distance of your kicks is inconsistent, you are probably not pushing aggressively enough with your plant foot. To be consistent with the height and distance of your kicks, you must focus on pushing consistently and aggressively with your plant foot. If you vary the amount of push with your plant foot, the height and distance of your kicks will also vary.

Once you have achieved consistency with your plant foot push, you can learn to control the flight of the football. This is because you will be imparting similar energy to the football, causing it to fly similarly from kick to kick. Before you can attain mastery over the flight of the football, you must first learn to make a consistent push with your plant foot.

Pushing aggressively with the plant foot will also reduce the number of short or *mis-hit* kicks. If you push with your plant foot as described, you can be assured of transferring the most possible energy to the football. Thus, even mis-hit kicks will have a better chance of traveling high, far, and straight enough to be successful.

A NOTE TO KICKERS

The football scoring system awards a team no additional points for how far a kick travels beyond the goalposts. So avoid the temptation of thinking you have to kick the football far to be judged a good kicker. Concentrate first on being accurate and put distance second, and you will always have a chance of being the kicker for whatever team you are on.

THE SAME NOTE FOR COACHES

Avoid the temptation of thinking that your kicker has to kick the football far to be effective. Coach your kickers to be accurate first and de-emphasize distance. Adopting this strategy will ensure having a kicker who can kick winning field goals and extra points when your team needs them.

Besides, how many times have you tried a 50-yard field goal to win a game? How many times have you tried a 42-yard field goal or less to win a game? If you look at this statistic over your years of coaching, I think the answer will be obvious!

Coach for accuracy, and distance will come as a result of perfecting the kicking technique—and you will win football games!

chapter 2

TEAM KICKING OBJECTIVES

Most coaches think that every placekicker should be able to kick the football through the uprights on command. While this may be true, it is not exactly why you are learning the skill of placekicking. You are learning to kick accurately and correctly to help your team win football games.

Many individuals can kick a football high, far, and straight. Few do it well enough to help their team win games. As you learn to kick correctly, keep in mind the explicit reason you are learning the skill— so your team wins the game. If you have any other reasons for learning how to kick you will inhibit your ability to reach your maximum potential and your selfishness will ultimately be your demise.

As Vince Lombardi so aptly stated, ". . . any man's finest hour— his greatest fulfillment to all he holds dear—is that moment when he has worked his heart out in a good cause and lies exhausted on the field of battle—victorious."

It is your job to incorporate your kicking skills into the production of an extra point, a field goal team, and a kickoff team to make it an effective unit. It is not the job of the other players to fit into what you want them to do for you. You have the easiest athletic responsibility of the 11 players on those special teams. Do not proclaim that it's hard and do not complain if things go bad. Simply focus and do what you have trained yourself to do—kick the football through the uprights.

This chapter on team kicking objectives is designed to give you and your coach ideas for incorporating a successful kicker into a productive special team. However, remember that it is up to you to make yourself a productive part of the special teams.

EXTRA-POINT AND FIELD-GOAL KICKING

Coaching the snap-to-kick time is more than simply telling a kicker he has to get the kick off in a specified time. It includes coordinating and evaluating the protection, the snap, and the holder to determine the best time for each kicker to perform in. Often the kicker is given a predetermined time established as "the time" in which an extra point or field goal must be kicked and is asked to adjust to that time. Traditionally, this time has been 1.3 seconds from snap to kick.

The error of thought in not incorporating other parts of the extra-point and field-goal operation, as well as individual variation from kicker to kicker, in establishing performance criteria for the snap-to-kick time is that the predetermined time may actually contribute to the kicker not performing to the best of his ability. It may be a time that is too fast for him to kick the football effectively.

No player on the team will have as many opportunities to win the game as the kicker. If any player on the team should have the best possible conditions to perform in, it should be the kicker. It is not that he is any better or deserving of special attention—but on his foot will often rest the success of the entire organization, the happiness of the alumni and fans, and even the coach's job itself.

Coaches must make a philosophical decision on whether to continue using a predetermined time for each kicker, and make the kicker adjust to that time, or to maximize the kicker's ability and fit it into extra-point and field-goal protection. In many cases, it is merely a matter of allowing the kicker a few hundredths of a second longer to kick the football to maximize his ability.

The faster the kicker must approach the football to kick it within the allotted snap-to-kick time, the more efficient his technique must be to control the distance and accuracy of his kicks. Kickers should not be rushed through their approach to the football until they have developed some technique efficiency to kick it where they want it to go. Otherwise, a kicker will have doubts about his ability to perform! Good coaches know that nothing is more damaging to a player's performance than doubting himself.

To begin with, the kicker should be allowed 1.5 seconds from snap to kick and should work down to the standard 1.3 seconds most coaches desire. He should practice this over a two-week period and take part in drills prior to team time to learn what this speed feels like.

During this period, the coach and the kicker should NOT be concerned with kicking results. Accuracy and distance do not matter. If a kicker is fairly competent before learning to go faster to approach the football, he will not lose his kicking ability. It is more important for a kicker to develop a feel for the speed at which the coach wants him to go. Over numerous repetitions, the increased approach speed and his kicking ability will all come together.

By focusing on the line blocking while the kicker is taking longer than 1.3 seconds to kick the football, coaches will see that the line can protect longer than 1.3 seconds and that the kicker gets his optimum kicks off between 1.35 and 1.40 seconds.

Determining the Snap-to-Kick Time

Essential to coaching any sport is accurate knowledge of how each player is developing. By closely monitoring each player's practice repetitions, a coach can develop a fairly accurate assessment of how they will perform on game day. A coach can obtain the same knowledge of how the kicker will perform by charting his kicks in practice. Charting a kicker during practice is a coach's tool for learning what level of performance he can expect from his kicker.

To obtain specific information on kicking time, the coach should observe the kicker giving a maximum performance and use the elapsed time from the center snap to the holder's catch to compute an average snap-to-hold time. In addition, he should note the range of snap-to-hold times—slowest and fastest—to assess the degree of impact the center has on total snap-to-kick time. For example, if the kicker's time appears slower than normal, do not assume the kicker has changed his speed to the football; it could be the center snap that has slowed.

As the kicker kicks, the coach should chart the time from snap to kick and note when the kicker hits his best kicks (table 2.1). A minimum of 20 well-hit kicks is needed to have an accurate snap-to-kick time for the kicker. After charting 20 well-hit kicks, the best snap-to-kick times should be grouped to find the average time the kicker needs to perform maximally. In addition, the worst kick times should be averaged and any difference in times noted.

Averaging each kicker's snap-to-kick time and knowing the influence of the snap-to-hold time will give the snap-to-kick time that is the best for *that* kicker, not an arbitrary number. Use the best and

Table 2.1

SNAP-TO-KICK TIME CHART

Date:____ /____ /_____

Kicker: _____

Center snap-to-hold time (sec)

1) _____.43_____
2) _____.45_____
3) _____.41_____
4) _____.45_____
5) _____.42_____
6) _____.43_____
7) _____
8) _____
9) _____
10) _____

5

6   1   3

2

4

*chart location of each kick
(if desired)

Snap-to-kick time* (sec)

1) _____1.33 _____
2) _____1.32_____
3) _____1.35_____
4) _____1.27_____
5) _____1.35_____
6) _____1.25_____
7) _____
8) _____
9) _____
10) _____
11) _____
12) _____
13) _____
14) _____
15) _____
16) _____
17) _____
18) _____
19) _____
20) _____

Ball hit (Good or No Good)

1) _____G_____
2) _____G_____
3) _____G_____
4) _____NG_____
5) _____G_____
6) _____NG_____
7) _____
8) _____
9) _____
10) _____
11) _____
12) _____
13) _____
14) _____
15) _____
16) _____
17) _____
18) _____
19) _____
20) _____

Average snap-to-hold time: _____ .43 _____

Average snap-to-kick time of good kicks: _____ 1.34 _____

Range of kick times from worst to best: ___ 1.25 - 1.35 _____ worst snap-to-kick times to determine a range of time in which the kicker should perform.

By monitoring the speed of the kicker's approach, a coach can discern the kicker's needs and coach the protection accordingly. Too often, coaches place the burden of preventing the kick from being blocked on the time it takes the kicker to kick the football. The snap-to-kick time should not be viewed as a block time, but merely as a barometer of the time required for the entire kicking unit—snapper, holder, and kicker—to operate successfully. If a kick is blocked, it is generally due to poor protection.

A coach can directly manipulate how long his kicker has to kick the football by how much emphasis he places on coaching protection at the line of scrimmage. The coach of a quarterback who is not particularly agile and a little slow with his drop-back steps would coach his offensive line to protect longer so the quarterback would have extra time to throw the ball. The same should be true for the kicker. A coach should give the kicker the opportunity to perform to the best of his ability by placing emphasis on teaching the line-of-scrimmage blockers to protect for as long a time as the kicker needs to perform maximally, within reason.

By adopting this placekicking strategy, a coach will feel he has more control over the outcome of the kick, and the coach, the kicker, and the entire team will feel more confident when the extra-point and field-goal unit goes out to perform.

KICKOFFS

Many coaches look for a kicker who can kick the football into the end zone consistently. As much as they hope to find such a kicker, the reality is there are few who can perform this skill as consistently as coaches would like. Additionally, statistics show that teams score less than 3 percent of the time when they start their possession inside the 20-yard line and 12.5 percent of the time from the 20-yard line. How can you increase your chances of stopping your opponent after the kickoff or make them start inside the 20-yard line if your kicker kicks it into the end zone every time?

It is more realistic to find a kicker who can consistently kick the football inside the 5- to 10-yard line with acceptable hang time. By understanding what to expect from a kickoff, a coach can focus more on teaching coverage and less on coaching the kicker to kick it into the end zone every time or recruiting the "one in a million" kicker who can do that.

Ideally, coaches would like to have the kicker kick off inside the five-yard line with a four-second hang time. Although these are appropriate kickoff goals, many kickers are never able to achieve them. A good high school kickoff will be inside the 15-yard line with 3.3 to 3.6 seconds of hang time. A good college kickoff will be inside the 10-yard line with 3.5 to 3.8 seconds of hang time. With proper physical and technical training, these are times that high school and college kickers can be expected to achieve consistently.

A popular assumption regarding kickoff coverage is that the greater the hang time, the better the coverage by the kickoff team. However, there is no direct correlation between the height of the kick and the effectiveness of the coverage, as many coaches assume. Good kickoff coverage is a product of factors that do not include the height of the kick.

The speed with which the coach can get the coverage team to sprint downfield, the techniques coverage players are taught to avoid blockers, and their ability to idle down their speed to make one-on-one tackles are the determining factors of good kickoff coverage. Although additional height on the kickoff can contribute to better kickoff coverage, poor coaching of kickoff coverage techniques will result in poor kickoff coverage far more often than a kickoff with marginal height. Asking the kicker to kick the football higher will not make the kickoff coverage better. Only teaching better coverage techniques will do that.

Kicking Off to a Corner

Another method of improving kickoff coverage is to have the kicker kick off to one corner of the field. This tactic reduces the amount of field the coverage team must cover, allowing them to converge on the football more quickly. It also makes the return man move to catch the football, because most return teams do not align a return man in the corner of the field. Forcing the return man to move to catch the football complicates the catch and keeps him from catching the football and starting directly upfield, threatening the kickoff coverage.

When kicking to a corner, the aim for the kicker is to place the football inside the 10-yard line and between the numbers on the field and the sideline. Distance becomes less important when kicking to a corner because the location of the kick provides the coverage team with advantages that overcome lack of depth. In other words, the location of the kick is more important than the depth of the kick. As a rule of thumb, the high school kicker should be able to get the football inside the 15-yard line and the college kicker inside the 10-yard line.

To kick to the corner, the kicker can align the football in the middle of the field or on a hash mark. There are no advantages to placing the football in either position on the kickoff, although some coaches would argue that by placing the football in the middle of the field, the kicker can disguise which corner he is kicking to.

If coaches commit to kicking off to a corner, the kicker should practice from both locations and use the one he is the most comfortable with and can execute the corner kick from the best. Remember, location is paramount to successful coverage of a corner kick, so choose the location from which the kicker can execute the corner kick most successfully.

Kicking Onsides

Everything to this point has been focused on explaining how the soccer-style placekick is performed correctly. Kicking an onsides kickoff is the one instance where the kicker must perform the placekick incorrectly. Typically, the coach wants a "squib" kick or a rolling end-over-end kick toward the sideline. For both these types of kickoff, the football must be contacted with an abnormal technique and in a spot other than the sweet spot.

The Squib Kickoff. A squib kickoff looks like a knuckleball and bounces in different directions when it hits the ground. This type of kickoff is used when the opponent has a good return man and the coach wants to keep him from fielding the kickoff cleanly and returning it. The squib kickoff is classified as an onsides kickoff because the objective is not to kick the football deep, but rather for it to travel to about the 25- to 30-yard line and bounce erratically. This tactic gives the kickoff coverage team a chance to run downfield and make a play to recover the football or tackle the return man as soon as he touches the ball.

To perform the squib kickoff, use your normal kickoff approach steps to run to the football. Typically, the coach will want the squib kick to go to one side of the field, so you may have to realign yourself to kick to the left or right. The adjustment you must make for the squib kickoff is to use more of a sweeping swing with your kicking leg, rather than a descending and ascending swing, and contact the football above the sweet spot or in the middle. The follow-through of your leg will be lower, and you want to drive the football more downfield than into the air by pushing more downfield with your plant foot.

When performing a squib kick, you should not use an easy leg swing. The coach does not want the kick to be too short, and the easier your leg swing on the squib kick, the fewer random bounces the football will take and the less distance it will go downfield. The aggressiveness of your leg swing should remain the same as for a normal kickoff.

The Sideline End-Over-End Onsides Kickoff. The more common onsides kickoff is the rolling end-over-end sideline kick that is aimed toward one sideline and takes a high bounce, giving the kicking team an opportunity to recover it. The success of this kick depends on the kicker's ability to aim the football so that it travels at least 10 yards downfield and rolls end-over-end rapidly to produce the high bounce. A kicker can become adept at performing this onsides kickoff with minimal practice.

To perform the sideline end-over-end onsides kick, align yourself facing in a direct line with the sideline toward which you are kicking. You need not go back very far to perform this kick. Two to three yards back and five to six yards toward the target sideline is a typical approach distance for this type of kickoff. You should experiment with the approach distance to find the optimum and comfortable place for you to start this onsides kick.

Once you have reached your starting point, choose an aiming point for the onsides kick that is 15 yards downfield and on the sideline closest to where the football is teed. This may be a certain player, coach, manager, or whoever or whatever happens to be at that point. This is the point you will run toward and swing your leg toward to direct the football down the field.

To execute the sideline end-over-end onsides kick, contact the top third of the football with your toe, your instep, or the sole of your kicking foot. The contact point for high school and college kickers is the white ring on top of the football. You should push hard through this spot to enable the ball to go the entire distance to the sideline. The impetus of a swing with this objective will produce a rolling end-over-end kick with a high bounce two-thirds of the way to the sideline.

If you have developed some competency at kicking a football, you can practice the sideline end-over-end onsides kickoff once a week for five to eight repetitions and execute this kickoff well enough to give your team a chance to recover it when necessary. You do not need to practice onsides kickoffs with any more than this frequency or number of repetitions.

The success of an onsides kick is mostly due to a fortunate or lucky roll of the football. Therefore, as long as you can kick the football to the proper depth on the field with the proper spin or rotation, you have done what is required for the onsides kick. You will be much better off practicing and honing the proper placekicking techniques rather than investing time becoming good at onsides kickoffs.

Using table 2.2 will guide you through the process of coaching yourself after a bad kick. Stay calm, cool, and collected through the learning process—others will be anxious enough for you. Always remember to keep your team kicking objectives firmly entrenched in your thoughts. You are a *team* kicker, not a kicker who is on the team. Otherwise, you may become a kicker who needs a team.

Table 2.2

ASK THE COACH	
What's wrong with my kick?	**How do I correct it?**
My kick misses to the left.	• Point your plant foot toe directly at the target. • Swing straight through the football. • Keep your upper body vertical. • Swing smoothly. • Check for correct plant foot position. *Practice drills:* One-Step, Goalpost, Kicking at One Upright Drills
My kick misses to the right.	• Point your plant foot toe directly at the target. • Keep your upper body vertical. • Snap your knee to accelerate your leg through the football. • Attack the football with an aggressive swing. • Check for correct plant foot position. *Practice drills:* One-Step, Goalpost, Kicking at One Upright Drills
The ball spins fast and high, but lacks distance.	Move your plant foot farther back and swing aggressively up through the ball. *Practice drills:* No-Step and One-Step Drills
The kick is a low line drive.	• Move your plant foot farther up on the football. • Position your upper body more vertical. • Snap down at the football from the knee. *Practice drills:* One-Step, Goalpost, Kicking at One Upright Drills
The ball spins like a propeller, not end over end.	Make sure your swing is balanced and your body is moving toward the target, not falling off to the side. *Practice drills:* No-Step and One-Step Drills
I hit the tee or the ground with my foot.	Move your upper body behind the football by adjusting your plant foot back. *Practice drills:* No-Step and One-Step Drills

Table 2.2 (continued)

ASK THE COACH	
What's wrong with my kick?	**How do I correct it?**
The kick lacks distance.	To increase distance • make a smooth, rhythmical swing; • explode up through the ball with your foot while making precise contact with the ball; and • generate more leg speed by pushing more aggressively with the plant foot. *Practice drills:* Dry Run and One-Step Drills
The kick lacks height.	Do not sweep the ball off the tee, but snap down through it from the knee. *Practice drills:* One-Step and Goalpost Drills
The ball spirals off the tee.	• Snap down and up into the football. • Move your plant foot closer to the tee. • Keep your body balanced on your plant foot as you swing. *Practice drills:* No-Step and One-Step Drills

chapter 3

PRACTICE DRILLS FOR PLACEKICKERS

There are many drills you can use to develop your kicking skills. It is important to have a core of drills to rely on for your development, since having too many drills may actually hinder it. Select one drill that develops one or two particular aspects of the kick and master that drill and that aspect of the kicking mechanic.

While variety may be the "spice of life," it can be a disaster for sport skill development. You will only improve a skill through repetition of it in the same drill and setting. Changing drills randomly or intermittently is not necessarily a productive decision.

The essence of improving your performance using these drills is hard work. The drills in themselves do not make you better. It is the intensity, commitment, and concentration of your work habits as you do the drills that will ultimately determine your success.

Doing the drills three times a week as you train will become tedious no matter how experienced you are as a kicker. This is a natural process and one where the best kickers reaffirm their commitment to their goal and trudge forward.

Be sure to set a performance goal and stick to it. Remind yourself of it daily, weekly, monthly if necessary. A saying we have used to motivate kickers is "Anyone can be average. Be the best!" It takes no additional effort, work, or planning to be average. All you have to do is show up and do what is expected. The best show up and do the expected, give the extra effort, and do the work no one else wants to do. That is what makes them the best!

Purpose:

This drill is used to practice the entire kicking motion without kicking the football. It is an excellent warm-up drill that all kickers should do to loosen up prior to a training session or a game kick.

Procedure:

You should align yourself, assume your stance, take your approach steps, and swing your leg exactly as if you were going to kick the football, only there is no football for you to kick.

a

b

Key Points:

Use a tee or a spot on the ground to mark where the football would be. Keep your eyes focused on the spot as you swing your leg through and simulate kicking the football. Do 10 dry-run repetitions as warm-up to full-speed kicking.

c

d

Purpose:

This drill works on developing the ability to transfer your leg swing momentum from your plant leg and foot into and through the football. It forces you to kick using whole-body mechanics and not just your leg by pushing with your plant foot through the football.

Procedure:

1. Position your plant foot next to the football, exactly where it should be on contact depending on whether you are kicking off a two-inch tee, a one-inch tee, or the ground.
2. Place your kicking foot behind the football.
3. Shift all your weight onto your kicking foot, then rock forward and transfer the weight to your plant foot.
4. As you transfer the weight from your kicking foot to your plant foot, raise your kicking leg and swing and kick the football.

Key Points:

Use your plant foot to push your body past the football on contact for maximum transfer of your leg-swing and body momentum to the football. No steps are used to kick the football because your plant foot is already positioned.

Text Review:

Leg Swing for a Soccer-Style Kick, pp. 18-23; *Body Movement Technique Checklist,* p. 23; *Plant Foot Technique Checklist,* p. 23.

ONE-STEP DRILL

3

Purpose:

This is a good transition drill from the No-Step to the Dry Run Drill. It focuses on proper plant foot stepping and positioning, which are essential for good ball contact.

Procedure:

1. Start with your kicking foot slightly in front of where you would be on your drive step to kick the football using your normal steps—one step back and one step over from the tee.
2. Leaning forward in a good starting stance with your weight on your kicking foot, push off your kicking leg and step with your plant leg to plant your foot.
3. Swing your leg and kick the football.

Key Points:

The One-Step Drill is identical to the No-Step Drill except you are allowed to take one step with your plant leg. Two sets of 10 kicks should be done when training.

Text Review:

Your Plant Foot During the Leg Swing, pp. 21-22; *Plant Foot Technique Checklist*, p. 23.

Purpose:

This drill is used to develop the proper height on the football so it cannot be blocked at the line of scrimmage. It is a good drill for improving the height of kicks.

Procedure:

1. Tee the football using a holder or holding device seven yards from the goalpost.
2. Using your normal extra-point and field-goal kicking steps, try to kick the football over the crossbar.

Key Points:

Use caution during this drill, because if you hit the crossbar, the football will bounce back at you at a high rate of speed. Keep your head down on the follow-through and prepare to be hit if you hit the crossbar with the football. The holder should protect himself also.

Text Review:

Maximum Height and Distance, p. 32.

KICKING AT ONE UPRIGHT DRILL

Purpose:

This drill develops straightness of form, accuracy, and directional control of the football.

Procedure:

1. Place the football 10 to 15 yards from and directly in line with one of the two uprights.
2. Kick the football using the proper techniques so that you can hit the upright.
3. To do this, you must make good contact, push your body through the football, and follow through to the target.

Key Points:

This advanced drill can tell the kicker what level of mastery he has of the kicking skill. It should be done once a week for two sets of 10 repetitions. The kicker will be amazed how wide the goalposts look after kicking at a four-inch target.

Variations:

This drill can also be done by kicking at a telephone pole, a spot on a wall, or any other object, if you do not have access to goalposts. In addition, you can stand in the back corner of the end zone, where it meets the sideline, and kick at the upright from the side angle. The end line and the lines on the field help you align yourself visually with the goalposts from the spot of the kick.

Text Review:

Leg Swing Contact Point, pp. 19-20; *Your Plant Foot During the Leg Swing*, pp. 21-22; *Swinging Your Leg After Ball Contact*, pp. 28-30.

Purpose:

This drill works on preparing the kicker for a last-second field goal attempt, specifically, when he must run onto the field and kick without the time to set up and get ready.

Procedure:

1. Place a football on the field at the line of scrimmage from which the football is to be snapped.
2. The kicker, the holder, and the snapper should stand on the sideline waiting for the coach's command.
3. On the coach's command, the three should run on the field as quickly as possible and kick the field goal.

Key Points:

The coach should tell the kicker, holder, and snapper how many seconds are left in the game and then count them down out loud as they run onto the field. Practice this from the left and right hash marks and the middle of the field. Allow the kicker 18 seconds to get the kick off when going from your bench to the far hash mark, 15 seconds when going to the middle hash mark, and 12 seconds when going to the near hash mark. These are minimum amounts of time for a field goal team to run onto the field and get a kick off from those areas of the field.

Variations:

The coach can use this as a team drill by adding the offensive line and wingbacks and making the entire extra-point and field-goal team run onto the field to kick the winning field goal.

Text Review:

Determining the Snap-to-Kick Time, pp. 37-39.

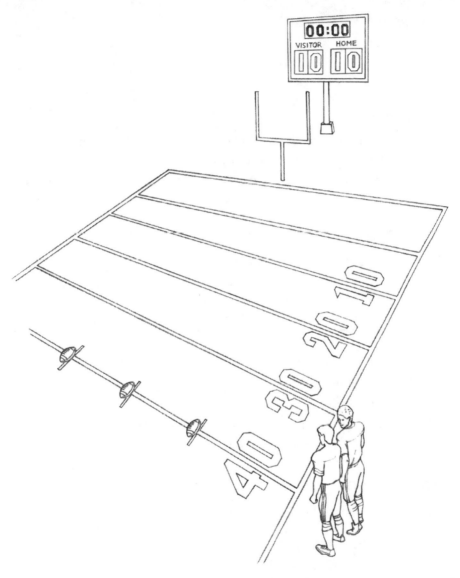

7

BAD HOLD DRILL

Purpose:

This drill will help develop your mental confidence and toughness by placing you in situations where things are not perfect but you must still make the kick.

Procedure:

1. The holder places the football on the tee or holds in any manner he chooses except the proper position.
2. You must go through your kicking steps and kick the football through the goalposts.

Key Points:

Do this once a month for 10 kicks.

Variations:

1. laces facing toward the kicker
2. football on the end of the tee
3. football on the front of the tee
4. football leaning too far backward
5. football leaning too far forward
6. side of the football on the tee, rather than the point
7. holder lets go of the football before contact

Text Review:

Extra-Point and Field-Goal Kicking, pp. 36-39.

8

LINE DRILL

Purpose:

This drill tells you how much control you have over the flight of the football. When done regularly, it develops control of the kick.

Procedure:

1. Tee the football on a line that runs across the field.
2. Kick the football using your normal steps.
3. When you are finished, check for two things before you move. First, you should have finished your swing and be standing to the side of the line. Second, the football should have landed farther across the field but on the line or within one yard to either side of it.

Key Points:

If the football does not land in the suggested area, you made a technique error in the swing, plant foot push, or body balance. Correct the error and repeat the kick.

Variations:

You can do this drill from the back of the end zone and kick at the goalposts from the side.

Text Review:

Your Plant Foot During the Leg Swing, pp. 21-22; *Balancing the Finish*, pp. 30-31.

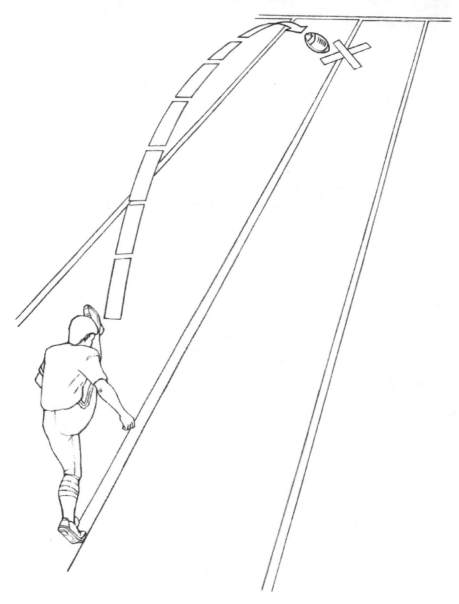

Purpose:

This drill works on developing accuracy by reducing the width of the goalposts for the kicker to kick at.

Procedure:

1. Place the football at the intersection of the 15-yard line and the sideline.
2. Kick the football through the uprights.
3. If the kick goes through the uprights, move down the sideline toward the end zone at a predetermined increment. I recommend moving five yards at a time until you get to the goal line, then moving down the sideline at two-yard intervals. You must make the kick from each distance prior to moving down the line.

Key Points:

Placing a limit on the number of kicks prior to the drill puts pressure on the kicker to go as far as possible down the sideline.

Variations:

Play this as a game, like "Around the World" in basketball. If the kicker misses, he can use a "chance" for an extra attempt, but he must go back to the beginning if he misses the chance kick. Do this with a group of kickers and alternate turns. You can also play this like "Horse." Each miss earns the kicker a letter. Once he spells H-O-R-S-E, he is out. Allow the kickers to choose the location of each kick instead of going straight down the sideline.

Text Review:

Leg Swing for a Soccer-Style Kick, pp. 18-23.

chapter 4

PUNTING TECHNIQUES

Whenever an athlete embarks on learning a new skill, he must have a goal or a philosophy as to why he wants to learn that skill. Without a goal, philosophy, or statement of purpose through which the athlete can filter the various concepts, techniques, or suggestions presented to him, he will become an experiment rather than a developing athlete. In simpler terms, an athlete can spend all his time becoming a "jack of all trades and master of none."

Punting the football has two simple objectives: The punt needs to travel high and it needs to travel far. Thus, techniques, ideas, or suggestions that do not affect either the height or the distance of the punt can be left to the punter's individual preference or will prove to be insignificant in teaching the skill. Techniques that affect the athletic position are considered height- or distance-affecting techniques.

My philosophy for teaching punting centers on techniques that relate specifically to the height and distance of the punt. Understanding the techniques that directly control these two variables will help you master the skill and enable you to control your performance. Where individual technique preference is permitted, it will be noted. Additionally, I will describe how the techniques being explained affect the height or distance of the punt.

REFERENCE POINTS AND COACHING PHRASES

When teaching a new skill such as punting, it is important to use descriptive terms that are easily remembered so the athlete can quickly recall the information. Specific reference points and coaching phrases enable the athlete to coach himself, if necessary, and give a coach specific techniques to cue on for adjustment and mastery of performance. Additionally, specific teaching terms permit the coach and athlete to communicate using a vocabulary that is unique to the skill of punting.

The sequence for teaching the punting skill is also important. The sequence should begin with those variables that have the greatest affect on the height and distance of the punt and progress to the individual preference techniques. A sequenced plan of instruction ensures the punter of progress toward improving his skills and enables the coach to evaluate any punter's level of development and move him from that point forward. A proven instructional sequence for teaching the skill of punting follows.

PUNTING INSTRUCTIONAL SEQUENCE
Ball-Drop Techniques
Leg Swing Techniques
Ball Contact Points
Stance
Approach Steps
Situation Punting

Learning an athletic skill cannot be a long trial-and-error process. The athlete's timetable for development is short. Mastery of the skill can be achieved with a proven sequence of specific instructional phrases, drills, and a teaching schedule.

ALIGNMENT DEPTH

Your alignment depth must be deep enough to avoid making it easy for the opposing rushers to block the punt but not so deep that the distance is difficult for the snapper to snap. A depth of 12 to 13 yards for a high school punter and 14 to 15 yards for a college or pro punter will align the punter back far enough to avoid the easy punt block yet remain within the normal distance a center can snap effectively at each level.

A punt cannot be executed without first getting the snap to the punter. If the snapper is not well skilled in snapping techniques or strong enough to get the football to the punter at the appropriate distance, the punter should move forward to ensure a clean snap and catch. More time should be spent coaching protection to adjust for a decrease in the punter's depth from the line of scrimmage.

Determining the Alignment Depth

Once the coach has determined your proper alignment depth, it is your job to align not only at the proper depth but straight behind the center. If you inadvertently offset your alignment to the left or right, the center will have to snap the football at an angle and the opposing rushers will have a shorter distance to go to block the punt.

To align properly, you must first find the proper depth by counting yardage from where the football will be snapped. Once you have positioned yourself at the proper depth, find the snapper and align your body directly behind him and in line with the football. In addition, your hips, shoulders, and knees should be facing straight ahead and square to the line of scrimmage.

When you come in from the sideline, watch where the ball is downed on third down and run onto the field 10 yards from where it will be spotted. With this method, you only count three to five yards for depth alignment and are less likely to make a mistake in counting. If you are a position player on offense and then must punt, you will have to count from where the football is spotted to get your alignment depth.

This scenario typically occurs at the high school level. It's a good idea to have a coach monitor your alignment from the sideline to ensure that you have counted right and are aligned at the proper depth. At times, as a position player, you can become so focused on playing your position that the details of alignment escape you.

If you have aligned at the wrong depth, the coach who is watching your alignment from the sideline can tell you to move forward or backward as appropriate. Alternatively, he can stand on the sideline at the proper depth so that you can simply look at the sideline and align yourself at that depth.

Alignment Procedures

❏ Find your alignment spot by counting back from where the football will be snapped.

❏ Go back 12 to 13 yards from the line of scrimmage if you are a high school player and 14 to 15 yards if you are a college player.

❏ Align yourself directly behind the snapper.

❏ Stand with your hips, shoulders, and knees facing straight ahead.

THE PUNTER'S STANCE

The stance a punter assumes has distinct characteristics. Because you may have to move to your left, right, jump to catch a high snap, or bend to field a low snap, you must be in the athletic position. The athletic position refers to having your shoulders over your knees, your knees over your toes, and your feet shoulder-width apart to establish a good base of support for movement.

The athletic position permits efficient movement in any direction because the body angles—hips, knees, and ankles—are bent and balanced around its center of gravity. This position allows you to move immediately to field a misdirected snap with no wasted motion. You can step, jump, or bend directly to your position without first having to move in a direction other than the way the football is misdirected by the snap.

The athletic position is used for most other football positions in which the players are standing on two feet. For example, linebackers, defensive backs, wide receivers, and running backs who are standing up all use some variation of the athletic position for quick and efficient movement. Linebackers and defensive backs will bend more at the knees, whereas wide receivers and running backs will bend more at the waist in the athletic position. However, they will all have their body angles bent so that the shoulders are over the knees and the knees are over the toes.

Finding Your Stance

You must be comfortable when aligned to receive the football. You should stand with your feet shoulder-width apart. If your feet are farther apart or closer together, you may have to take a false step before punting the football to put your feet in shoulder-width position. This is because having the feet shoulder-width apart is the most naturally efficient position for body movement.

The toes of your feet can either be parallel or your punting foot can be offset in a toe-to-instep relationship (figure 4.1). Use personal preference when deciding how to position your feet, as long as you remain in the athletic position.

Figure 4.1 Punter's foot spacing in the stance.

If you are a three-step punter, you will generally have your feet parallel or your nonpunting foot forward. If you are a two-step punter, you will generally align with your punting foot slightly forward of your nonpunting foot or have your feet parallel. You should be able to align and punt from either of these stances, because there are punting situations where each type of stance is beneficial for your performance. For example, all punters should use a two-step stance when punting out of the end zone.

Positioning Your Body for the Stance

In your punting stance, your body weight is forward on the balls of your feet. This allows you to move forward efficiently to punt the football. You should bend at the waist and knees so that your shoulders are leaning forward over the top of your feet, in athletic position (figure 4.2). Your arms should hang freely in front of and away from your body in a ready position to receive the snap from the center. Your palms should be facing forward to provide a target for the center snap. Your head should be up and your eyes focused on the center snap.

Figure 4.2 Punter's body position for the stance.

At this point, you should be focused on catching the snap. Your thoughts should be on making good, solid contact with the football. You should not be thinking about technique, adjustments, field conditions, weather conditions, and so on. You should clear all of these thoughts from your mind and focus only on catching the snap and contacting the football as solidly and precisely as possible.

The training you have done to perform the right techniques during the game will take effect without consciously having to recall it. In fact, the more conscious you are of performing the right techniques, the less likely you will be to do so. You must learn to focus your mind on catching the snap and contacting the football to be able to punt consistently well and develop command of the skill.

Stance Technique

❏ Stand with your feet shoulder-width apart. Your feet should be in a toe-to-instep relationship or parallel, and your body weight should be forward on the balls of your feet.

❏ Bend at your waist so your shoulders are over your knees.

❏ Bend your knees so that they are over your toes.

❏ Let your arms hang freely in front of your body with your palms facing forward.

❏ Keep your head up and your eyes focused on the center snap.

THE SNAP AND POSITIONING OF THE FOOTBALL

Catching the center snap is the single most important punting skill you must possess. If you cannot be counted on to catch the football cleanly, you cannot be the punter. Because the punter must stand 13 to 15 yards behind the line of scrimmage as the football is traveling toward his team's goal line, a coach will not play a punter he cannot trust to catch the snap. Dropping the center snap at any time, in practice or a game, leads to distrust with coaches. It simply cannot be tolerated and must be eliminated through practice repetitions and drills.

Although catching the center snap is not a difficult physical skill, it must be practiced and rehearsed with the right mental attitude. You must take pride in catching the snap and expect to be able to catch any type of snap, good or bad, that comes your way. Additionally, you cannot use a bad center snap as an excuse for a poor punt. If you do not credit the snapper for your success when the snap is good and you punt well, then you should not blame him when the snap is bad and you punt poorly.

All situations, good or bad, should be viewed as ones that need to be practiced and mastered so that a good performance can result under any conditions. The proper mental approach to catching the center snap is to take full responsibility for fielding the snap, regardless of whether it is good or bad. Once this mind-set has been adopted, you have taken the first mental step toward command of the skill.

Receiving the Center Snap

The center snap should be received with your hands away from your body. You must reach out to catch the center snap at arm's length with your elbows slightly bent, as if you were a receiver catching a pass (figure 4.3a). You must not catch the football with any part of your body except your hands (figure 4.3b). If the football touches any other part of your body, chest, stomach, upper or lower arms, you will waste time repositioning it in your hands before extending it outward to punt it.

Figure 4.3a Catching the center snap.

Figure 4.3b An improper catch of the center snap

Once you have the football in your hands, keep it at arm's length and rotate it quickly so that the laces face upward. The football should stay in this position, at arm's length with the laces facing upward, throughout the rest of the punting mechanics.

Adjusting to Misdirected Snaps

You must be able to move laterally, bend low, and jump to catch misdirected snaps. In these situations, your first thought must be to keep your body in front of the football. Using specific adjustments for each situation makes it easier to field the ball cleanly and still make your normal smooth, rhythmical approach to punt the football.

Every punter must be capable of fielding a misdirected snap and still executing a good punt. Punting the football after catching misdirected snaps must be practiced, and you must have the expectation of being good, not only when the snap is good, but also under bad snap situations. The best punters do.

When the center snap is misdirected to your left or right, you should shuffle your whole body in front of the football. Reaching to the side to catch a punt increases your handling time because you must twist your body back to face squarely downfield. Reaching to field a laterally misdirected snap is also not conducive to keeping your body in front of the ball.

At the same time, you must be determined to do whatever it takes to prevent the football from going past you. If that means reaching with your arms instead of sliding your body to field the football, then reach!

When the center snap is low or on the ground, bend at your knees and waist to block and scoop the football. Position your hands in front of and between your legs to prevent the football from rolling between your legs. As your palms are already facing forward, focus on keeping your rear end low while the football is low, and raise it only if the ball bounces or rises from the ground. This technique is the same one a baseball infielder uses to field a ground ball.

By bending at your knees, hips, and waist in your stance, you are already set to jump to field a snap that is too high for you to reach. When you must field a high snap, you should extend all your bent joint angles and jump as high as possible to catch it.

When you return to the ground, speed up your steps to punt the football as quickly as possible. The high snap has given the rushers extra time to block the punt, because it will take you more time to get the football in position to punt it. At this point, how the punt looks is unimportant; your main priority is to give your opponent the football from a punt, not as the result of a punt block. Just make sure to get the punt off.

Receiving the Center Snap Technique

❑ Catch the snap with your hands at arm's length from your body and your elbows slightly bent.

❏ Keep the football at arm's length and rotate it so that the laces face upward.

❏ Shuffle your body laterally to catch laterally misdirected snaps.

❏ Bend at the waist and knees and lower your rear end to receive low snaps or snaps on the ground.

❏ Jump to field high snaps by extending your bent body angles.

❏ Keep your body in front of the football in all situations.

VERTICAL BALL-DROP POSITION FOR THE PUNT

Catching the center snap allows you to *execute* the skill of punting. Correctly dropping the football to be punted allows you to be *successful* at the skill of punting. In other words, how the football is presented to be punted, or the position the ball is in as a result of the ball drop, determines how high, far, and straight the punt travels.

Being able to drop the football in a position to ensure the punt travels high, far, and where you want it to is *the* primary punting mechanic that must be mastered to be successful. Being able to present the football properly from the ball drop is what separates average punters from good punters and good punters from great punters. You cannot punt the football high, far, or straight if you cannot consistently drop the football in the proper position.

An analogy that underscores the importance of the ball drop is that of a batter in baseball. The single factor that determines the success of the baseball batter is the location of the pitch he chooses to hit. The batter must rely on the ability of the pitcher to throw the baseball in the strike zone so that he can hit a pitch in the best location to maximize his batting abilities. If the batter is a .300 hitter when he hits balls that are in the strike zone, he is less than a .300 hitter when he hits a ball that is outside the strike zone. This is because he must make an adjustment in his mechanics to hit a baseball that is out of the strike zone.

The same relationship is true for punting. When the punter swings his leg to contact the football, he is like the batter. When the punter drops the football to be punted, he is like the pitcher. A punter who continually drops the football wrong is like a batter swinging at bad pitches. He cannot perform to his maximum ability because he must make an adjustment in his punting mechanics to punt the poorly dropped football. Conversely, a punter who is adept at dropping the football has the opportunity to perform to his maximum ability on a consistent basis.

The primary difference in this analogy is that the baseball batter has to rely on someone else—the pitcher—for his success. The punter is able to be both pitcher and batter. Because the punter pitches to himself, it is within his control to always have a good ball drop to punt. A punter who cannot drop the football properly cannot be a good punter.

Gripping the Football

To drop the football properly, only three gripping methods should be used: placing your hand on top, underneath, or on the side of the football (figures 4.4 a-c). Any of these hand positions is acceptable as long as your grip is the same each time and the presentation of the football adheres to the requirements necessary for a good football drop position.

The hand position I will discuss and teach in this text is the hand-on-the-side position. This position is favorable for punters with small fingers and young punters between the ages of 10 and 14 who are learning to punt a large football for the first time. The grip, arm position, and other handgrip techniques related to this hand position are specific to gripping the side of the football and cannot necessarily be used with the other hand positions.

Figure 4.4a   Hand-on-the-top grip position.

Figure 4.4b   Hand-underneath grip position.

Figure 4.4c   Hand-on-the-side grip position.

The football should be held with your fingers spread and the butt end of the ball in the palm of your hand. The pressure to hold the football comes from your fingertips. Do not touch the football along the length of your fingers or with the palm of your hand. The football should feel comfortable in your hand, and you should be able to hold it out in front of you without feeling as if it is going to fall out of your hand. If you do not feel comfortable with your hand on the side of the football, you should try the other hand positions until you find a comfortable grip.

As previously noted, the football should be held so that the laces face upward. When holding the football on the side, your middle finger is the hand reference point and the side seam of the ball is the football reference point. Knowing the location of your middle finger relative to a landmark on the football will ensure that you are holding the ball the same way every time. These reference points will also serve as coaching points to check in case you are having trouble with dropping the football.

The middle finger of your drop hand is either on top of, parallel to and above, or parallel to and below the seam that is on the outside of the football. The back tip of the football is in the palm of your hand, and your fingers are spread comfortably around the back end of the ball. Your fingertips, not the palm of your hand or the surface of your fingers, are applying the pressure when gripping the football.

Positioning Your Wrist

Your wrist should be held in a *hand-shaking position*. To find this position, grip the football, hold it straight out, and drop it without moving your hand or arm. Your hand should be in a position to shake hands with another person (figure 4.5). If it is not, adjust your wrist position and repeat the steps. In essence, you are shaking hands with the football as you hold it to drop it for the punt.

Figure 4.5 Hand-shaking wrist position.

The position of your wrist affects how much the nose of the football is angled inward. The degree of inward turn affects the optimal flight path of the football. The more you angle the football inward, the more difficult it is to make it turn over in a spiral. Also, if you vary the amount the football is turned inward from drop to drop, you have little chance of being in control of the flight of the football. Using the hand-shaking position keeps your wrist and the inward turn of the football consistent each time you drop the football.

Angling the Front End of the Football

I am often asked about the degree of inward turn the football should have so it will spiral or turn over. Not only is it impossible to determine the exact amount of inward turn for the football, it is also impossible for you to adjust the ball visually to the appropriate angle when you have only 2.2 seconds to punt it. Thus, visual keys such as the degree of inward turn are impractical for performing, teaching, or monitoring proper drop techniques.

A practical physical reference point such as the hand-shaking position provides you with instant feedback on the correctness of angling the football. It also provides the coach with a technique that can be filmed and evaluated for effectiveness. However, for informational purposes, the amount of inward turn of the football for optimal flight and turnover is 10 to 15 degrees.

The football must be dropped in line with and over the top of your punting leg. The line your punting leg travels on when your foot swings up from the ground to contact the football and continues through the follow-through is on a plane referred to as the *vertical swing plane*. To ensure efficient contact and transfer of energy from your body and kicking mechanics to the football, the ball must be dropped in the same vertical plane as the path of your punting leg. The position of the elbow of the arm dropping the football plays a significant role in determining the vertical plane in which the football is dropped.

Positioning the Drop Arm

To properly position your drop arm, use your *drop arm elbow* as your reference point. Your drop arm elbow should point directly at the ground and be in line with the hip of your punting leg (figure 4.6). This position, along with the hand-shaking wrist position, angles the football inward correctly and positions it in the proper vertical plane (figure 4.7).

Figure 4.6   Inside position of the football in the hand.

Figure 4.7   Proper position of drop arm elbow.

You must not try to place your drop arm elbow over your leg. As you are holding the football on its side, holding your drop arm elbow over your leg will position the ball too far inside of your punting leg, or too far inside the proper vertical plane.

Dropping the football inside the proper vertical plane is similar to a pitcher throwing the baseball inside to the batter. The batter can never get his arms fully extended and put maximal power or bat speed into contacting the pitch. The same is true for a punter. When you drop the football inside the correct vertical plane, you cannot put any power into the punt because you must redirect your swing or turn your body to contact the football. Both of these adjustments produce less than maximal energy to transfer to the punt.

Factors Affecting the Vertical Position of the Ball

A common mistake punters make is turning the drop arm elbow outward. Turning the elbow to the outside affects the inward angle of the football and changes the vertical plane in which the football drops. The outward-positioned elbow causes the football to angle too far inward because it rotates the wrist and forearm inward. In addition, when the elbow turns out, it moves the football inside the vertical drop line.

To illustrate how the elbow position affects the drop position of the football, hold the ball with the correct grip and drop arm position and extend it out to arm's length. Position the drop arm elbow facing the ground and note the location (vertical plane) the football is in. From this position, turn the elbow outward and watch how the football moves nose inward and physically inward. This should be a vivid example of why proper positioning of the drop arm elbow is so important.

Using the Ball-Flight Location to Determine the Vertical Ball-Drop Position

The directional flight of the football is an indicator of the vertical ball-drop position. For the football to have a straight flight path, the vertical ball-drop position must be directly over the top of your punting leg. If you punt the football when the ball is dropped inside your punting leg, it will go to your left. If you punt the football when the ball is dropped outside your punting leg, it will go to your right. In either case, the football will not travel as high, far, or straight as needed to be an effective punt.

When you have dropped the football inside or outside the vertical drop line, you need to make an adjustment before your next punt. Move the football farther out or farther in, depending on the directional flight of the ball. If the football flies to your left (right-footed punter), move the ball farther outside because you dropped it too far inside. If it flies to your right, move the ball farther inside because you dropped it too far outside.

Adjusting from punt to punt is necessary to develop the proper techniques for positioning the football to be punted. Do not continually punt footballs left or right without making a ball-drop adjustment. It will do nothing to improve your command of the skill.

Vertical Ball-Drop Technique

❏ Hold the football with your fingers spread and the butt end of the football in the palm of your hand. The football is held with fingertip pressure, not with the palm touching.

❏ Grip the football with your middle finger on top of, parallel to and above, or parallel to and below the seam on the side of the football.

❏ Keep your wrist in *hand-shaking* position and your drop arm elbow pointing directly at the ground.

THE BALL DROP

The horizontal positioning of the football, whether the nose is turned up, down, or remains flat, affects the precision of contact between the punter's foot and the ball. To transfer maximal energy to the football, the contact between the ball and your foot must be solid and precise. Otherwise, some of the energy is lost in the collision and not transferred to the ball. If you cannot drop the football flat, any superiority you have in other punting techniques will be negated. Contacting the ball well as a result of dropping the football flat is a critical step in becoming the best punter possible.

Dropping the Ball Flat

To transfer energy to the football to produce height and distance, the ball must be dropped and contacted when it is flat. If it is contacted by your foot when the nose is up or down, it is not being contacted in the optimum spot to travel through the air in an aerodynamic spiral. In either of these contact positions, your foot is contacting a smaller part of the football than if the ball were dropped flat and contacted in the middle.

When the football is dropped with the bottom parallel or flat to the ground, the middle or widest part will be exposed to your foot as it swings to contact the ball (figure 4.8). For maximal transfer of energy to take place, your foot must contact the middle of the football. This can only happen if the football is dropped flat or parallel to the ground.

Figure 4.8 Flat ball drop.

To ensure that the football is dropped flat, you must control the bend in the wrist that is holding it. As the football is held in hand-shaking position, your wrist should also be held straight out with no upward or downward tilt. Tilting your wrist up or down causes the nose of the football to tilt up or down when it is dropped. Neither position will produce a good punt because the football is not flat.

Holding your wrist straight is not a natural position. You must be physically and visually conscious of your wrist in the correct position before you can recognize whether or not you are keeping it straight as you drop the football. You must master the skill of keeping your wrist straight as your hand and arm lower to drop the football.

Lower the Football for the Drop. The drop arm elbow and wrist must lower the football simultaneously without bending at their respective joints. If either joint bends, the nose of the football will turn upward or downward, and the ball will not be dropped flat. You must think of your drop arm as a single lever from shoulder to fingers that must not be bent.

Extend the Football Away From Your Body. Two factors affect how far the football is placed in front of your body before it is dropped: the bend in your drop arm elbow and the bend in your waist. The arm holding the football must be fully extended with a slight bend at the elbow (figure 4.9). Do not extend the arm so that you hyperextend the elbow or tense the muscles. This prevents you

Figure 4.9 Drop arm extension and starting height for ball drop.

from dropping the football smoothly and controlling the speed of the drop. The slight bend in the elbow prevents the muscles from contracting or becoming rigid.

If you stand straight and extend your arm while holding the football and then extend your punting leg outward, you will see that the football does not reach your foot if only your elbow is fully extended. If you were to drop the football and punt it from this position, you would have to lean backward because the ball is not extended far enough to be dropped over your foot.

However, if you bend at the waist so that your shoulders are over your toes, the football will be extended the extra distance necessary for you to drop it over your foot. If you bend at the waist and do not fully extend your drop arm elbow, it will have the same affect as not bending at the waist at all. The football will not be far enough in front of you, and you will have to lean backward to punt it.

If your elbow is fully extended and you are bent at the waist, the football will be a consistent distance from your body each time you punt it. This is because the length of your arm will not change and the bend in your waist can be attained consistently. This is important for establishing a consistent drop point at which you can contact the football.

Any variation in the distance the football is dropped in front of your body will cause your body position to vary when you punt the ball. As a result, you will have little control over the height and distance of your punts.

Positioning Your Upper Body

At some point in the punt you must be balanced on one leg, so the position of your upper body is important because it affects your balance. Bending your waist and shoulders over the toes puts you in the athletic position as you drop the football. This position must be maintained as you release the ball (figure 4.10). Do not lean backward when you drop the football.

The position of your upper body during the drop phase is the initiator of your upper body position for the leg swing. Positioning your shoulders incorrectly during this phase of punting contributes to being in a bad position for the next two phases of the punt: the leg swing and contact with the football.

Figure 4.10 Upper body position for the ball drop.

Starting Height of the Ball Drop

Before the football is dropped to be punted, it must be raised to a maximum height. This position is termed the *starting height* of the ball drop. The starting height of the ball drop is important because it directly influences how high off the ground the football is contacted. This then determines the height and distance of the punt. Therefore, you must know the proper starting height for the ball drop and how to position the football there for each punt.

You must not move the football up or down while you are taking your steps or you will unconsciously vary the starting drop height from punt to punt. Varying the starting drop height varies the height and distance of the punt. To ensure that a punt will have the height and distance you intend it to, you must learn to keep your drop arm at the same height as you take your steps to punt.

As mentioned previously, your goal is to learn techniques, perform drills, and train to develop *command* of the punting skill. This means that you are progressing toward competency in duplicating the correct punting techniques punt after punt. Mastering the skill of dropping the football from a consistent and proper starting height is the first step in developing control of the height and distance of your punts.

The proper starting height for the football is chest high across from the nipples when your arm is fully extended. Your drop arm should stay in this position as you take your approach steps. When viewed from the drop arm side, a punter's drop arm should remain at the same height throughout his steps.

When the football is raised to chest height to be dropped, it does not actually feel as if it is at chest height (figures 4.11a-b). Because you

Figure 4.11a-b　Ball height during steps.

a

b

are bent at the waist in the athletic position, it feels as if the football is as high as your head. This feeling is normal, and coaches should reinforce that this is exactly how it should feel. As long as the football is at chest height when viewed from the side, it is in the proper starting height position, regardless of what it feels like.

Speed of the Ball Drop

The punter controls the speed with which the football drops from his hand toward the ground. The faster you allow the ball to drop toward the ground, the less time you have to swing your leg through and punt it. This causes you to rush through your mechanics and lose your rhythm and smoothness, resulting in a poor punt.

Learn to drop the football softly, as if it were a baby you were going to lay on the ground. Drop it flat so the middle is exposed for optimal contact, and learn to release your grip gently so as not to disturb the inward angle. These are the factors that control the speed with which you drop the football.

Develop a consistent drop speed under all circumstances. Typically, when you are rushed by your opponent, you will quicken your drop speed, rush through your mechanics, and likely produce a poor punt. Keeping the speed of your drop consistent and not allowing the rush of your opponent to hasten your punting mechanics is a mental challenge. Perform numerous repetitions in a rushed setting to convince yourself that speeding up your ball drop is unnecessary.

The higher the ball is dropped from the ground, the more time it has to accelerate due to the pull of gravity and the impetus or push from the drop hand. Thus, you want to minimize the time the ball spends in the air without being held or punted. Your ability to control the "free" air time of the football relates directly to the speed of the ball drop.

Control the speed of the ball drop by holding the football and guiding it downward from the starting height position. The ball drop is *not* made from the starting height position. Initiate the ball drop by guiding the football six to eight inches down the vertical drop line *before* releasing it (figure 4.12). This reduces the amount of free air time for the football and controls the speed of the ball drop.

If you catch the center snap, raise the football to the starting height, and drop it immediately, it will drop very quickly. When you neglect to keep the football at the starting height during your steps, your drop hand will have the tendency to push the football downward, causing it to drop too fast instead of slowly and gently.

Figure 4.12 Guiding the ball down the drop line.

Release the Football. Releasing the football so that it travels downward in the same alignment position as it was when held in the hand is a skill that separates average punters from good punters. The football must be released smoothly and gently so the nose does not turn inward or straighten and the ball remains flat as it drops.

Until you develop some consistency in releasing the football from your hand so that it maintains the proper drop position, you should not swing and contact a football. Conversely, if you can become adept at releasing the football and having it maintain the proper drop position, you do not have to punt a lot of balls to improve your punting skills.

Release the football after guiding it six to eight inches down the drop line by spreading your fingers simultaneously away from and off the surface (figure 4.13). Your wrist should remain straight and firm as your fingers spread and your drop arm continues traveling down the vertical drop line toward your punting leg. If your wrist bends downward as the football is released, the nose of the ball will point downward as it drops. This is the most common mistake young punters make when learning how to release the football properly.

If released correctly, the football will drop perfectly flat and be in the exact position, laces facing upward, nose angled in, as when it was being held in your hand. If the football turns inward or straight-

Figure 4.13 Releasing the football for the ball drop.

ens as it drops, it indicates that your fingers did not spread smoothly or simultaneously from the ball. The reason is that as your fingers spread on release of the football, they actually hit the surface, causing it to turn horizontally in some way. The most common error in this release is for the football to remain flat but the nose to turn inward too much.

Envisioning a Point on the Football. In baseball, when a batter faces a pitcher who throws fast, it is often said that he "cannot hit what he cannot see." The same is true for the punter who hopes to contact the football in the proper location. As mentioned earlier, the proper location for contacting the football is on the bottom. Obviously, you cannot see the bottom of the football as it drops, so you must have a visual reference point on top of the football to enable you to contact the sweet spot on the bottom.

Ask a typical punter what he looks at as he punts the football and he will say "the whole football." This is one reason for not making consistent contact with the sweet spot. If a punter looks at the whole football, he will contact various parts of the bottom. Because the sweet spot of the football is in a specific location on the bottom of the football, to contact it you must have a specific visual reference point to focus your eyes on as the ball drops through the air.

The visual reference point on the top of the football that corresponds to the sweet spot on the bottom is located approximately one inch sideways toward the punter from the third lace. Each brand of football will have a name written in this area. Look at this location and select the letter that is in the position described. If you are using a Wilson football, you should use the letter "i" in Wilson as a visual reference point. You must keep your eyes focused on this location from the time you raise the football to the starting drop height, all the while it is dropping, until you contact the football.

In punting, a one-eighth inch mistake in contacting the sweet spot can make the difference between a good punt and a poor punt. Focusing your eyes on a specific spot will help you become a precise ball contactor. Although you may be able to correctly perform the essential skills of presenting and positioning the football to be punted, dropping and releasing it, and controlling the speed of the ball drop, failing to look at and hit the proper spot on the ball will negate the positive effect of those techniques. Training your eyes to find and remain on the proper spot on top of the football will ensure contacting the sweet spot every time.

Ball-Drop Technique

❏ Keep your wrist straight with no upward or downward tilt, so the football is flat.

❏ Lower the football in one motion, keeping your wrist and drop arm elbow straight throughout the drop motion.

❏ Keep your upper body in athletic position throughout the ball drop and as you take your steps.

❏ Raise the football to chest height—the *starting height* of the ball drop.

❏ Keep the football at chest height as you take your steps to drop the football.

❏ Control the speed of the ball drop by guiding the football six to eight inches down the drop line before releasing it.

❏ Spread your fingers away from and off the football simultaneously to release it for the drop.

❏ Keep your eyes focused on the spot on the top of the football that corresponds to the sweet spot on the bottom to make proper contact.

APPROACH STEPS

A punter must maximize every source of energy available to him for the football to achieve the maximum height and distance that correlates with his physical potential. Your resources for developing energy to transfer to the football are limited to the muscular power potential of your legs and hips, your level of punting technique efficiency, and the kinetic energy you acquire from stepping to punt the football. Of these three major contributors to the height and distance of the punt, stepping to punt the football permits you to use the physics of kinetic (moving) energy to impart greater height and distance to the punt.

Using Two or Three Approach Steps to Punt

You must be comfortable with the number of steps you take to punt the football. The smoothness and rhythm of your approach steps are significant in ensuring that you will transfer the maximum amount of kinetic energy to the punt. The coach should allow the punter to determine the number of approach steps that feels best for him.

There are two stepping patterns to choose between in determining the number of steps you will use to punt: a two-step approach or a three-step approach. Try both stepping patterns and determine which feels most comfortable or natural, and then use that stepping pattern to punt on a regular basis. Eventually, you will have to learn to use both a two-step and a three-step approach for certain situations. However, for normal punting situations, use the number of steps you feel most comfortable with.

Most punters are three-step punters. The extra momentum generated by this approach translates into greater leg speed to punt the football. Also, most punters say the three-step approach feels more natural. The two-step approach tends to be more mechanical and less rhythmical, yet it must be learned, because you cannot use the three-step approach when you have to align less than 14 yards behind the center. Although each stepping pattern is useful in certain punting situations, with the proper repetitions and training, neither pattern is more advantageous than the other for normal punting if performed properly.

In stepping to punt the football, keep your body in the athletic position. Your upper body should remain motionless as you take your approach steps (see figures 4.14a-c and 4.15a-e). Any movement of the upper body during the approach steps changes the direction of the kinetic energy and reduces the amount your approach steps can generate.

Take normal walking-length strides or steps during the approach. Longer approach steps will cause you to lean backward as you step to punt. Conversely, if your stride is too short, the large muscles of your hips, buttocks, and thighs will be unable to contract maximally to generate power in your steps. As a rule, your steps should cover a distance of four yards or less.

During your approach steps, your weight should remain on the balls of your feet. This will enable you to push forward to your toes on each step, as if walking down the street. Keeping your shoulders in athletic position and your upper body motionless during your approach steps helps keep the weight on the balls of your feet.

Do not begin your approach steps until *after* you catch the football. You must be stationary *as* you catch the football. Stepping forward to catch the center snap forces you to handle it perfectly. It also prevents you from reacting laterally to a misdirected snap because you will always be stepping straight ahead.

Begin your steps *after* you catch the football from the center snap and *while* you are raising it to the ball drop starting height. If you step to catch the center snap and raise the football to the ball drop starting height at the same time, you will be forced to handle and rotate the ball perfectly to execute the punt. By not allowing a margin for error, you will affect your team negatively if you are unable to handle the ball.

These general approach step techniques are applicable to both methods of stepping to punt the football. Either method can be used effectively by any punter. As mentioned previously, personal preference, comfort, and performance capability should be the criteria for selecting the number of steps you take to punt the football.

Two-Step Approach. In the two-step approach to punting, you take your first step with your punting foot and a second step with your nonpunting foot and then swing your leg to punt the football. This stepping pattern must be learned because it must be used when you are standing less than 14 yards behind the center to punt. This situation occurs when you are punting from your own end zone with the football placed inside the five-yard line.

To perform the two-step approach properly, put more weight on your nonpunting foot in your stance. This allows you to push off this foot after you receive the center snap. When your weight is evenly distributed on both feet, you have to lean or shift your weight to the side of your nonpunting foot before you can push off to take your approach steps. Shifting your weight while in your stance facilitates the two-step approach and decreases the time you must handle the football (figure 4.14a-e).

Figure 4.14a-e Two-step approach sequence.

a

b

c

Figure 4.14a-e Continued

d

e

Three-Step Approach. When using the three-step approach, take your first step with your nonpunting foot and your second step with your punting foot. Your third step is with your nonpunting foot. Although this approach may seem to require too much time to punt the football, remember it is the quickness of your feet, not the number of steps you take, that determines how fast the football is punted.

The first step in the three-step approach is a short weight-shifting step six to eight inches in length. It allows you to transfer your body weight forward more so than if you had your weight on your toes while in your stance. The second step in this approach, the drive step, should be of normal stride length and allows you to gain maximal body speed for transfer of energy into the punt. The third step is the plant step (figure 4.15a-f). The third step is slightly longer than the drive step because you have greater body speed while taking this step, forcing a longer than normal stride.

Figure 4.15a-f Three-step approach sequence.

a

b

Figure 4.15a-f　Continued

c

e

d

Figure 4.15a-f Continued

f

If you take your first weight-shifting step as the football is traveling from the center, you are actually a two-step punter because you will only be taking two steps to punt after you catch the ball. This stepping pattern is a nice compromise if your coach forbids or does not like you taking three steps to punt the football, yet you feel more comfortable and can punt better using the three-step approach. This technique can only be used when the snap is good.

Stepping the Approach Path

The path you take with your steps to punt the football is referred to as the *stepping approach path*. This left, right, or straight-ahead approach path of your steps affects your leg swing path. It also determines the part of the football you will contact. Even though the inward angle of the nose of the football may be correct and the football is positioned in the correct vertical plane, if your stepping approach path is misdirected, your leg swing will not contact the proper spot on the football. The result will be a short miscontacted, or shanked, punt.

Walk straight ahead and not to the left or right to punt the football. If you hold the football in the prescribed position, a straight stepping approach path will position your leg swing on a path to contact the middle of the football. A stepping approach path that is to the left causes your leg swing to contact the front end of the football. A stepping approach path that is to the right causes you to contact the back end of the football. In either case, your foot will not contact the desired sweet spot.

A straight stepping approach path is not natural. Most punters have a natural tendency to walk to the right to punt the football. Although you can punt effectively with an approach path that wanders to the right or left, it is not advisable because it is difficult to walk at the same angle every time. Thus, you will not be walking toward the same part of the football to make contact each time, which means you will be an inconsistent ball contactor.

To step in a straight line, you need a landmark to get yourself moving straight. When you catch the snap from the center, point the football at the center and begin your approach steps toward the front end of the football or toward the first of the laces. These landmarks help ensure you are stepping down a straight path to punt the football.

Approach Steps Technique

❑ Use steps that are comfortable for you to punt the football.
❑ Use either a two-step or three-step approach.
❑ Keep your body in athletic position as you step to punt.
❑ Keep your upper body motionless during your approach steps.
❑ Take normal walking-length strides.
❑ Keep your weight on the balls of your feet as you step.
❑ Cover no more than four yards with your approach steps.
❑ Remain stationary as you catch the center snap.
❑ Begin your approach steps *after* you catch the center snap and *while* you raise the ball to the starting ball height.
❑ Take your approach steps in a *straight line*.

FOOT-TO-BALL CONTACT POSITION

The contact between the foot and the ball controls the aerodynamic flight of the football. The most advantageous flight position for the football to travel in is a spiral. A spiraling football is able to minimize the resistive effect of the elements—wind, rain, snow—on its flight. A nonspiraling punt can still be effective if it has good height and distance. However, unless the punt travels in a spiral, its height and distance will not reflect the maximum strength, technique, and ability level of the punter.

Learning how to punt a spiral is the culmination of the techniques described in this book. However, knowing what to do is often not the essence of learning. Knowing what caused the punt to *not* spiral, or to *not* go as high, far, or straight as desired, is the building block of attaining command of the skill. You must look at how the flight of the football appears for feedback that will indicate what technique errors you made that caused the football to travel in an undesirable way.

Knowledge of technique errors is the most important component in making adjustments. This knowledge permits you to coach yourself from punt to punt for continual improvement. With this type of self-coaching, you can be assured you are not repeating bad punts and are progressing toward command of the punting skill.

You must have a base of punting technique knowledge that permits you to understand why the punt looks the way it does. You must realize that it is you who controls and is responsible for the flight of the punt. If your punt lacks height, distance, or travels in an unintended direction, you made it do that as a result of some punting technique you did not perform correctly. If you can recognize the technique error that made your punt have less height, distance, or accuracy than intended and make an adjustment for the next punt, you are moving forward in your pursuit of having command over the height and distance the football travels.

Positioning the Football to Be Dropped

A few theories exist that attribute some significance to the location of the laces when you punt the football and its relationship to punting farther and higher. For example, one theory asserts that if you face the laces to the inside or outside so that the hole used to put air in the football points upward, you can get more height and distance on the punt because the bladder of the football opposite this hole is softer. I have not found this to be the case whatsoever.

Where you put the laces has no effect, positive or negative, on the transfer of energy from your body to the football when contact is made. Whether the laces face upward, sideways, or even straight down does not significantly affect the height or distance of the punt. The primary consideration for rotating the laces is to place them in a location where your foot does not contact them, because hitting them hurts the top of your foot. Rotating the laces upward after receiving the football ensures that you will not contact the laces.

Contacting the Football

Characteristics of the football's flight, such as direction, height, appearance, and whether or not it spirals, are a direct result of the precision of contact between the foot and the ball. There are three

Figure 4.16a-b
Contacting the middle of the football.

a

b

possible locations for contacting the ball: the front, back, or middle. To impart the maximum amount of energy to the football, it must be contacted in the middle (figure 4.16a-b). Contacting the front or back of the ball prevents maximum transfer of energy and results in a distinctly less than desirable flight direction and appearance.

Contact the football with the large bone on top of your punting foot, which is located directly under the shoelaces. Your punting foot toe must be pointed maximally so that a flat surface is presented from toe to ankle and up the shin. Keep your toe, ankle, and foot fully extended throughout the swing and during contact with the football.

Dropping the football parallel to the ground or flat will expose only the middle of the football to the foot. A double contact often occurs when the football is not contacted in the middle. When the nose of the football is dropped upward or downward, your foot will first contact either the front or back of the ball and then milliseconds later will make contact at the middle. You will be unable to achieve the flat, precise contact necessary between your foot and the ball.

Positioning Your Body for Foot-to-Ball Contact

The position of your body on foot-to-ball contact affects the direction, vertically or horizontally, of energy transfer to the ball. Your shoulders act as a rudder for your body, steering the energy down the field for more distance (horizontally) or upward for more height (vertically). The desired position is for your shoulders to be leaning slightly forward and facing squarely downfield. They should remain in this position regardless of whether you are punting for hang time or distance.

Your upper body is approaching vertical or straight up and down as the football is contacted. Your head should remain motionless and down, with your eyes focused on the ball throughout the contact phase. If you keep your face down and your eyes on the football, your shoulders will continue leaning forward and be in the proper position throughout the foot-to-ball contact phase (figure 4.17). Lifting or bobbing your head during this phase causes your shoulders to lean backward, so that you lose control over the height and distance of the punt.

Figure 4.17 Body position on contact with the football.

Using the Appearance of the Ball's Flight to Determine Contact Points

When you contact a football that is not dropped flat, its flight takes on a distinct appearance that indicates whether the ball was dropped with the nose upward or downward. A nose-up ball drop results in the back of the football being contacted. This produces an end-over-end, tumbling punt. A nose-down ball drop results in the front of the football being contacted, producing a wobbly spiral. In either situation, because flat contact has not been made between the foot and the ball, the ball will not travel in a spiral.

A football that has been contacted on the back end will also tend to travel to the punter's left, instead of straight down the field, whereas a football that has been contacted on the front end will travel to the punter's right or off to the side. Using these flight reference indicators, you can recognize the error you made in the ball drop and correct it for the next punt. This will ensure that you do not repeat a mistake and are progressing toward mastery of the foot-to-ball contact skill. Table 4.1 summarizes the flight characteristics of miscontacted footballs.

Table 4.1

BALL FLIGHT INDICATORS			
Football angle at contact	Contact area	Flight appearance	Flight direction
Nose flat	Middle of football	Spiral	Straight ahead
Nose upward	Back end of football	End over end	Left of punter
Nose downward	Front end of football	Wobbly spiral*	Right of punter or off to side

*Degree of wobbliness depends on the degree of downward tilt of the drop.

Contacting the Football Technique

❏ Contact the middle part of the football.

❏ Contact the football with the large bone on top of your punting foot.

❏ Keep your punting foot toe pointed maximally during contact with the football.

❏ Make *flat* contact between your foot and the football.

❏ Keep your shoulders forward and facing squarely down the field on contact.

❏ Keep your head motionless and down, with your eyes on the contact spot of the football.

THE HEIGHT OF BALL CONTACT

How high the football is contacted from the ground determines the height and distance of the punt. If you learn to manipulate how far off the ground you contact the football, you will be able to punt for height, distance, or an equal combination of both on command. This is important when punting from different positions on the field and in weather conditions that necessitate punting the ball lower or higher to be effective. It is also important for punting strategically to put the opposing team at a disadvantage in either field position or being unable to return the punt.

The team-conscious punter learns to manipulate the height and distance of the football to increase the team's field position advantage. In addition, the punter who can control the height and distance of his punts can avoid having factors other than his own ability—weather conditions, for example—determine his success as a punter.

Controlling the Height of Ball Contact

The punting techniques that affect how high off the ground the football is contacted are the starting height of the ball drop, the release point of the football from your hand, and the speed of the ball drop. You must have some command of these skills to be able to manipulate the height and distance of the punt.

Using reference points for the height of ball contact provides you with visual awareness of where the punt must be contacted to control either the height or distance of the punt. Your nonpunting leg is used as the body reference point for the ball contact height landmarks. Do not use actual distance from the ground in feet or inches as a landmark. Monitoring distance from the ground makes it difficult to discern whether you have contacted the football two feet from the ground or two feet, four inches from the ground. Those four inches *do* make a difference in whether the punt travels higher or farther.

A visual landmark permits you to videotape yourself, stop the videotape at the moment of foot-to-ball contact, and discern whether the football is contacted in the proper location relative to the height landmarks. Each change in the desired result of the punt, height or distance, has a different landmark for the height of ball contact from the ground. Contacting the football at different height locations affects the part of the leg swing in which the ball is contacted. This, in turn, affects the height and distance of the punt.

Proper Height of Ball Contact. For the typical field punt, you need to punt the football with an equal measure of height and distance. To do so you must contact the football approximately two to four inches above knee level when you are standing straight. Thus, the reference point for producing a punt with an equal measure of height and distance is two to four inches above the knee of your nonpunting leg.

At this point, your leg swing is just above parallel to the ground, ascending, as it swings through to contact the football. Your body weight is on the toes of your plant foot which disperses the plant foot push upward (vertically) and forward (horizontally) so that some of the energy is transferred to both height and distance. There is never an absolutely equal measure of push for both height and distance, but contacting the punt at slightly above knee level produces as close to an even distribution as possible.

Contact Height for Hang Time. To produce a punt with more hang time than distance, contact the football at midthigh height or above. This permits contact to be made later in your leg swing, as it is rising (ascending) into the football. At this point, your plant foot is pushing more vertically than horizontally, resulting in more push for hang time than for distance.

To punt for hang time, you need to hold the football longer with your hand. Instead of starting the drop with your hand guiding the football six to eight inches down the drop line, you should keep the football stationary at chest height as long as possible. This allows your leg swing to move farther upward in its path before the football is dropped, and your leg will contact the football later in the swing.

When you make this punting technique adjustment for the first time, you will have the sensation that you are punting the football too high from the ground and that your leg is taking too long to swing through to contact the ball. It may even feel as if the football is at chest height when you contact it.

This feeling is natural and is to be expected when making this adjustment. Once you have done several repetitions making the hang-time punt adjustment, you will feel comfortable with the technique and be able to duplicate it on command. Knowing how to adjust for and execute the hang-time punting technique is important for punting to keep your opponent inside their own territory, coffin-corner or pooch punting, and punting the football to avoid any return.

Contact Height for Distance. To produce a punt with more distance than hang time, contact the football at knee height. This permits the football to be contacted earlier in the leg swing, before your leg is parallel to the ground and is in the early stage of its ascent into the football (figure 4.18). At this point, your weight is distributed evenly on your plant foot and you are able to push more horizontally than vertically, resulting in more push for distance than for hang time.

Figure 4.18 Contact point for a drive punt.

To punt for distance, hold the football longer as it drops down the ball drop line. Instead of guiding the football 6 to 8 inches down the drop line, guide it downward for 12 to 14 inches, or as long as possible. Also, bend more at the waist so your shoulders are farther out in front of your toes. This exaggerated athletic position helps ensure that the push of your plant foot is directed down the field.

The exaggerated bend of your waist also elongates the lower portion of your leg swing so that its ascending or upward path is not as abrupt. This allows you to contact the football during a part of your leg swing where its energy is directed more down the field than upward.

If you lean backward to perform this technique adjustment, you will flatten your leg swing too much and cause the football to be hit extremely low. In most cases, the result will be your typical shanked punt—very short, off to your right, and very low to the ground. To perform this technique properly, it is imperative that you stay bent over at the waist throughout the ball drop and ball contact phases. When the techniques for punting the football for distance are performed correctly, you can drive the football a long way down the field.

Once you have done numerous repetitions making the distance punting technique adjustment, you will feel comfortable with the technique and be able to duplicate it on command. You will then be able to punt for distance when you want to, not just by chance. This is important for punting into the wind and punting when your team is deep in its own territory.

As these two punting situations are extremely important in determining the outcome of a game, you must spend more time on perfecting the techniques of punting into the wind and punting from deep in your own territory than on any other technique adjustment. Mastering the punt for distance is one of the most important techniques you must learn to contribute to your team's success.

Punting for Height and Distance Technique

❏ For the *field punt*, contact the football two to four inches above the knee for equal height and distance.

❏ For the *hang-time punt*, contact the football at midthigh height for more height than distance.

❏ For the *hang-time punt*, hold the football at the starting drop height longer before you guide it down the ball drop line.

❏ For the *drive punt*, contact the football at knee height for more distance than height.

❏ To execute the *drive punt*, hold the football longer, for 12 to 14 inches, as you guide it down the ball drop line.

LEG SWING

Once you have positioned and dropped the football correctly, you must make a good, aggressive leg swing. The swing of your punting leg is the lever you will use to transfer all the strength and power from your body and the mechanical energy from your techniques to the flight of the football. Mechanical proficiency with the other techniques of the punt is useless if you do not execute a smooth, aggressive leg swing.

A good leg swing for the punt has several distinguishing characteristics. The punting foot is cocked and positioned to make a straight leg swing; the punting leg is fully extended on ball contact; the leg travels on a straight path before contact, at contact, and after contact; and the follow-through of your leg swings through to contact your chest in line with the eye on the same side as your punting leg. With knowledge of the proper leg swing characteristics and through periodic use of videotape, you can monitor your leg swing for technique errors.

Preparing Your Leg Swing

If you are a right-footed punter, your punting leg foot should be cocked behind your body as far as possible toward your right buttock (figure 4.19). Keeping your foot in line with your right buttock places your leg in a position to swing straight to the football. If your foot is cocked and over toward your left buttock, your leg will not swing straight and the football will not travel straight down the field.

Figure 4.19 Preparation of the leg for the leg swing.

The ability to make a straight leg swing allows you to have command of the directional flight of the football. Directional control of the punt is used for coffin-corner punting or punting away from the return man (directional punting). Without directional control of the punt, you will become a one-dimensional punter who is only able to punt the ball straight down the field.

If you can control the direction of your punts, you can be a strategic weapon for your team by punting the football in areas that minimize your opponents' ability to return punts and lengthen the amount of field they must move the football to score. In this capacity, you become a defensive weapon for your team, directly contributing to the effectiveness of the defense. In this team role as a punter, you can have a significant effect on the outcome of the game.

Leg Swing Contact Point. If your leg swing has been on a straight approach path to contact the football, your leg will be straight on contact. This is what will give you control over the directional flight of the football. If your leg follows a straight approach path, contact with the football is made as your leg is ascending. This is the point when you can impart the most energy to the football, or the *maximum velocity point* of your leg swing.

This point is reached just after your leg swing is parallel to the ground. At this point, the knee of your punting leg is locking out, your hips are beginning to roll or thrust into the punt, and the weight on your plant foot is being shifted to the toes to push your body through the contact point and down the field for greater height and distance on the punt. Coordination of these movements promotes maximum transfer of energy from your body to the punt to produce height and distance.

Body Movement During the Leg Swing. Your upper body plays a significant role in your leg swing. Moving your upper body too far forward or backward during the leg swing will negatively affect its path. Your upper body goes through three positions during the punting motion. First, the lean of your shoulders and bend in your waist are preset in the athletic position in your stance to receive the football. Your shoulders must remain in this position as you catch the snap and walk to punt the football. This helps direct your energy in the direction you are moving, straight down the field.

As you drop the football and begin the leg swing, your shoulders will move to the second position, which is slightly backward from vertical. This position readies or cocks your upper body for an explosive movement forward during the leg swing. You will not contact the football from this position.

The third upper body position is when you make contact with the football. At this point, your upper body will be in or approaching a vertical position, straight up and down. Being in a vertical position on contact with the football keeps your body balanced and readies your hips and plant foot to explode into the football.

As the football is contacted, your shoulders move forward and return to the athletic position to meet your leg, which is swinging through to punt the football. This forward movement enables you to use your plant leg to roll your hips and push your body through the football on contact. The explosion of your hips and plant leg enables you to use your entire body, not just your punting leg, to punt the football. This important mechanic is what makes the punt travel higher and farther.

If you lean too far forward as you punt, your leg will be unable to swing freely. This will shorten your leg swing path and inhibit coordination with and use of your plant leg for additional height and distance on the punt. A shortened leg swing also results in a tendency to contact the back end of the football rather than the middle. This is because your shoulders restrict your leg swing path and limit how far you can extend your foot, causing your leg to decelerate before it contacts the football.

If you lean too far backward as you punt, the ascending path of your leg swing becomes steeper, lengthening your leg swing. This changes the optimal contact point and puts your foot on a path to contact the front end of the football. Because you are leaning backward and your body weight is moving away from the contact point, the least amount of energy will be transferred from your punting mechanics. As a result, you will produce short, wobbly punts or shanked punts that fly off to your right.

The Plant Foot During the Leg Swing. The push of the plant foot contributes directly to the height and distance of the punt because it controls the speed and quickness of the hip and body explosion into the football. The more forceful or aggressive your push with the plant foot, the more quickly your hips and body will explode into the football and the higher and farther it will travel. It is also better to mis-hit a punt with greater hip and body explosion. An explosive body can transfer more energy to the football, giving it a chance to go high and far even if you mis-hit the punt.

An aggressive plant foot push will carry your body off the ground and well past the point where you contacted the football. If your body ends up about three to four feet downfield from where you made contact with the ball, you can be sure that you made a maximal push with your plant foot. Covering any less distance will result in a submaximal explosion of your hips during the leg swing.

The strength of your punting leg remains fairly constant from punt to punt. In addition, an experienced punter's mechanics do not change dramatically from punt to punt. What does vary is the aggressiveness of the plant foot push, contributing to variation in the height and distance of each punt. If you can make an aggressive, attacking push with your plant foot on a consistent basis, your punts will be more consistent and travel farther than if you are punting with leg strength only.

Leg Swing Technique

❏ Flex and cock your punting leg behind the buttock of your punting leg.

❏ Swing your leg in a straight path prior to, during, and after contact with the football.

❏ Lean your shoulders slightly backward prior to swinging your leg forward.

❏ Make contact with the football with your leg fully extended and your shoulders returning to vertical position.

❏ Contact the football when your leg is ascending to the *maximum velocity point*.

❏ Make an aggressive plant foot push.

❏ Keep your shoulders forward in athletic position after contact.

❏ Swing your leg through and contact your chest on the follow-through.

PUNT FINISH

How does the finish of your leg swing affect the height or distance of the punt? The answer is, it doesn't! Therefore, spending too much drill and instruction time working on the leg swing finish only serves to make you look better, not punt better. Even so, it is important for your leg swing to have a fluid and complete finish.

The finish of your leg swing involves the follow-through of your leg and the movement of your body after ball contact. By coordinating these two movements, you will complete the punt in control of your swing and be balanced when your punting leg returns to the ground. Proper execution of these techniques can be assessed by analyzing the finish of your body. This enables you to detect errors in those techniques that occur prior to ball contact.

Following Through

The follow-through of your punting leg allows it to maintain its speed and straightness through the ball contact point and permits it to decelerate safely and completely. The follow-through does not contribute to the hang time of the punt.

The follow-through has several distinguishing characteristics. First, your leg is completely extended with the toe pointed downward maximally—the same position it is in on ball contact. Second, your leg swings through the ball contact zone and upward toward your right eye. A slightly more rightward finish is acceptable, as long as the leg does not cross the middle of your body (figure 4.20).

Figure 4.20 Follow-through of the leg swing.

Any crossover of your leg swing in the follow-through indicates that it was not straight prior to and at contact with the football. As stated earlier, a straight leg swing is essential to controlling the flight of the football. Therefore, you must pay attention to the finishing path of your leg swing and not allow your punting leg to cross over during the follow-through.

Your leg must make a complete and fluid follow-through to ensure that it does not negatively affect the leg speed prior to ball contact. A complete follow-through is when your leg swings through the ball contact zone and upward until it comes in contact with your chest. This ensures that your leg maintained maximum speed through the ball contact zone. If your leg swing does not finish at your chest, it is decelerating when it contacts the football.

If your leg appears to stop on contact with the football, or you have little follow-through after ball contact, you need to develop more flexibility in your punting leg. This is a common deficiency in young beginning punters. A daily flexibility program will assist in developing the flexibility needed to make a longer leg swing and generate more leg speed.

Moving Your Body After Ball Contact

Once you make contact with the football, your shoulders and upper body move forward as a result of bending at the waist. This enables your punting leg to swing through to meet your upper body and keeps you balanced in athletic position throughout the contact phase, facilitating maximum transfer of energy into the football. Leaning backward or too far forward inhibits your body balance and disperses the energy away from the foot-to-ball contact. Eliminating this tendency is important because eventually you may move your upper body incorrectly *before* contacting the football, causing a misdirected or bad punt.

Once your leg has swung through and contacted your chest to complete the follow-through, it begins its descent to the ground. If your upper body has remained motionless as your leg completed its follow-through, you will be balanced and under control as your leg descends and finally returns to the ground. If you are not in control of your body and balanced at the finish of the punt, it generally indicates upper body movement during the leg swing. You must finish under control and in balance to have command of the punting skill.

Proper execution of the punting mechanics will produce straightness of form and motion in three essential areas: the approach steps, the ball drop, and the leg swing. The approach steps will be directed straight down the field, the football will be dropped straight over the punting leg, and the punting leg will swing straight up through the ball. Once the basic mechanics have been mastered, the effectiveness of your punting depends on how consistently you can keep these three areas in a straight line throughout the punting operation.

The difficulty of mastering straightness of form is what makes punting challenging and demanding. Achieving it even briefly at times is what encourages you to continue pursuing mastery of the punting skill. It is a shining example of why athletics can be rewarding and humbling, exhilarating and frustrating—all at the same time.

Punt Finish Technique

❏ Completely extend your leg with the toe pointed maximally.

❏ Accelerate your leg swing through the foot-to-ball contact phase.

❏ Swing your leg through to contact your chest for a complete follow-through.

❏ Move your shoulders and upper body forward to contact the leg swing.

❏ Keep your upper body facing squarely down the field throughout the follow-through.

❏ Stay balanced and under control as your leg descends to the ground.

THE HEIGHT AND DISTANCE OF THE PUNT

Performing the punting mechanics adeptly and in coordination with each other is the essence of what separates punters who can put great height and distance on the ball from those who cannot. Although body size and athletic ability assist in putting more height and distance on your punts, punting is primarily a fine motor skill that requires precise execution of the techniques to be successful, not absolute size or strength of body.

The essential elements of the punting mechanics that directly affect the height and distance of the punt are the ball-drop position, the height of ball contact from the ground, and the push of the plant foot. This does not minimize the importance of executing all of the punting mechanics correctly. It simply implies that you can have individual variation in performing some of the other punting mechanics, and even perform them incorrectly as you develop your skills, and still produce a punt with good height and distance, as long as these three essential elements are performed properly.

One theory suggests that a better follow-through of the punting leg contributes to increased height or hang time on the punt. However, once the football has been contacted by the foot, the energy has been transferred, and the ball is in flight, the follow-through can provide no other impetus to the ball. It simply functions to allow the punting leg to maintain its speed and straightness through the ball contact point and decelerate safely and completely.

A beginning punter should focus his training time on mastering the three essential elements of putting height and distance on the punt. Performing and mastering the drills that develop ball-drop positioning, height of ball contact, and push of the plant foot must be the starting point for all punters, whether you want to *control* the height and distance of your punts or *improve* the height and distance of your punts. Once you have become proficient enough to achieve consistency of technique at these skills, you can begin to work on maximizing your performance.

The two factors that determine the amount of power you can transfer to the football are the speed and strength of your punting leg. The kinetic energy generated by the steps you take to punt the football is what determines the speed of your punting leg. The amount of the plant foot push is what determines how much of that speed is transferred to the football. Becoming proficient with your approach steps and plant foot push will allow you to transfer the maximum amount of leg speed from your body movement to the football.

The strength of your punting leg does not change significantly from punt to punt until it reaches the point of fatigue. Developing the strength of your legs will permit you to make powerful leg swings longer. Instead of your leg tiring and losing strength after 20 punts, you can swing 35 times or more before your leg power decreases significantly. In addition, a stronger leg has more power potential. Consequently, making your legs stronger will also allow you to achieve a more powerful explosion into the football, resulting in greater transfer of flight potential—height and distance—to the ball.

chapter 5

SITUATION PUNTING

The factor that most determines the probability of the offensive team scoring is the location on the field where it takes possession of the football. The closer to the opponents' goal line the offense can take possession of the football, the greater their chances of scoring. The percentage of offensive scoring drives from various field positions is shown in figure 5.1.

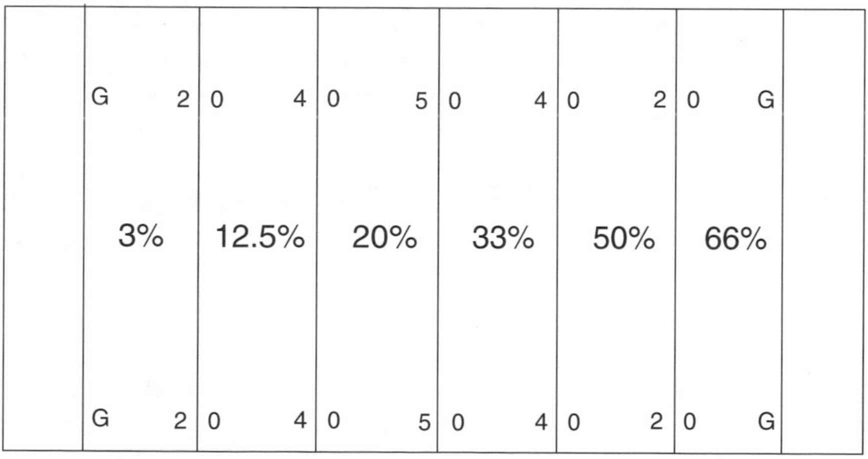

G 2 0 4 0 5 0 4 0 2 0 G
3%	12.5%	20%	33%	50%	66%
G 2 0 4 0 5 0 4 0 2 0 G

Figure 5.1 Percentage of offensive scoring chances for starting field positions.

Your primary purpose is to punt the football so that the opposing team's offense must drive as many yards as possible to score a touchdown. You cannot do this successfully if each time you take the field your sole objective is to punt the football as high or as far as possible. Different locations on the field dictate that you must punt the football with more height than distance or more distance than height. Field punting position also dictates the need for punts to be directed to the sideline rather than straight down the field.

To be the quintessential *team* punter, you must learn to be a situation punter. A situation punter is one who takes the field knowing what type of punt is best for the field location of the football and then has sufficient command of the punting skills to perform that type of punt. If you punt the football as high and as far as you can in every situation, you are only being self-serving and do not have your team's best interests in mind.

Being a situation punter means putting aside the traditional measure of a punter's effectiveness—the 40-yard average. This standard is meaningless to a situation punter. Each punt must be graded separately for its effectiveness in the situation from which it was punted. A plus and minus grading system similar to those the other position coaches use to grade their players is more appropriate.

A punt from the +40-yard line that travels 30 yards and goes out of bounds at the 10-yard line would be a plus for the situation in which it was punted. The same 30-yard punt from the +45-yard line that goes out of bounds at the 15-yard line would get a minus, because from that position on the field, the punt should be placed inside the 10-yard line. This creates a new standard of performance for the punter and maximizes his effectiveness for the team, not for himself.

SITUATION PUNTING FIELD POSITIONS

You must be able to perform four types of situation punts: *field punts, hang-time punts, drive punts,* and *coffin-corner punts*. Figure 5.2 shows the type of punt necessary according to the field position of the football. You must be cognizant of the field position of the football before you punt, determine the best punt for that position, and then execute it effectively.

Situation punting requires that you practice the four types of punts and not just punt straight down the field. Your punting practice repetitions must be allocated for each field position situation so that you are fully prepared to execute the necessary type of punt. For example, a practice session that requires you to punt 45 footballs might be allocated as follows: 10 field punts, 10 hang-time punts, 10

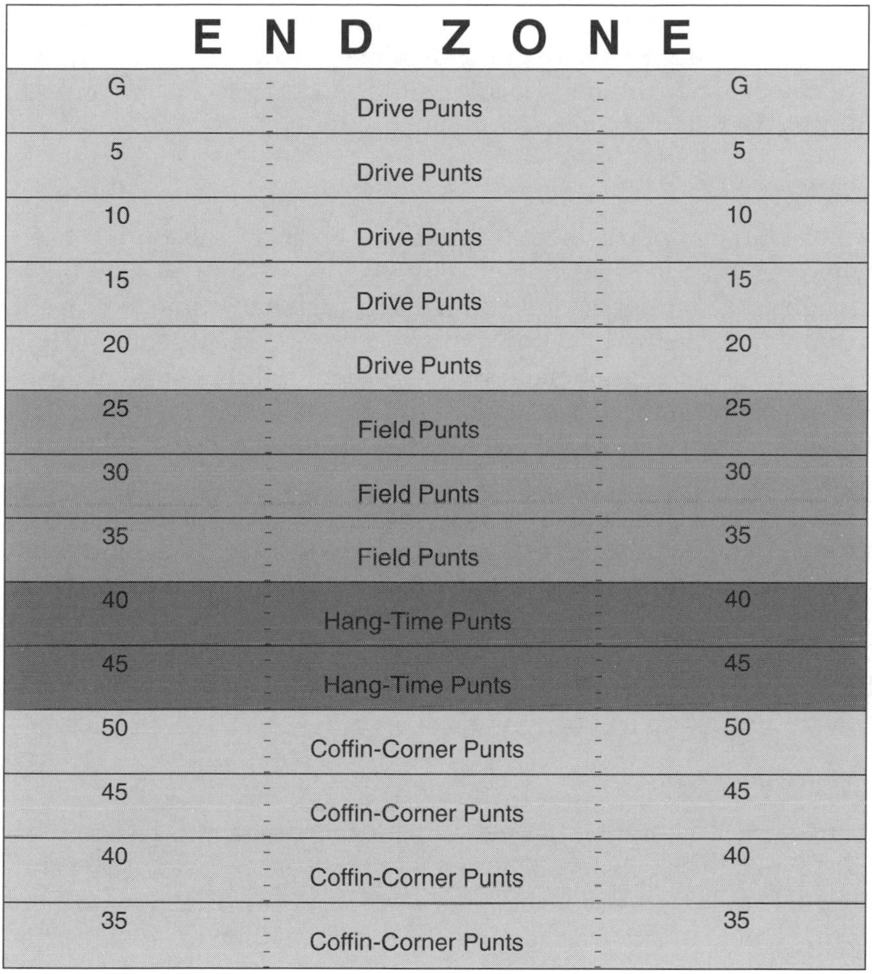

E N D Z O N E	
G	G
Drive Punts	
5	5
Drive Punts	
10	10
Drive Punts	
15	15
Drive Punts	
20	20
Drive Punts	
25	25
Field Punts	
30	30
Field Punts	
35	35
Field Punts	
40	40
Hang-Time Punts	
45	45
Hang-Time Punts	
50	50
Coffin-Corner Punts	
45	45
Coffin-Corner Punts	
40	40
Coffin-Corner Punts	
35	35
Coffin-Corner Punts	

Figure 5.2   Field-situation punts.

distance punts, and 10 coffin-corner punts. The other five punts will be at your or the coach's discretion as to which of the four areas you need additional work on.

Field Punts

A field punt is one with an equal measure of height and distance. This punt is used when the football is positioned between the –25- and –40-yard lines. In this field position, you are trying to punt the football with enough hang time to prevent a return but also with enough distance to lengthen the distance the opposing team must travel to score. In this field position situation, try for 42 yards on each punt and a net of at least 37 yards.

Hang-Time Punts

A hang-time punt has more height than distance. This punt is used when the football is positioned between the −40- and 50-yard lines. The object is to punt the football with enough hang time to prevent a punt return. In this field position, the opposition will generally line up to defend a possible fake punt, so there will be minimal rush. Thus, you have no excuse for not punting the football with enough height to force a fair catch by the return man and eliminate any return.

In this field position situation, you are the equivalent of a free-throw shooter in basketball. You are behind the center, and with minimal or no rush, you should be able to execute a hang-time punt with no return 85 to 90 percent of the time. If you cannot, it can only be for one of three reasons: lack of practice, not having command of the skill, or lack of mental concentration. If any of these is the case, the coach should find a new punter.

Drive Punts

A drive punt is one that has more distance than height. This punt is used when the football is positioned between the −25-yard line and the goal line. You want to get maximum distance on the punt to gain as much field position as possible for the opposition to defend. This is the most dangerous position on the field to punt from because your opponent will usually rush 10 men to either block the punt or make you speed up your punting rhythm and force a bad punt.

This is also the area where you can have the most negative impact on your team's chances of winning. A short punt in this field position allows your opponent to take possession of the football with only a short distance to go to score points. You must practice punting from this field position under rush conditions more than any other situation to maximize your chances of success in contributing to the team's effort when called on.

It is difficult to be successful in the minds of coaches when punting from this field position. Coaches want distance on the punt to get the ball out from deep in their own territory, yet they want height so the punt team can cover it. In essence, coaches want a 50-yard punt with 5 seconds of hang time, and you must catch and punt the football in 1.9 seconds or less because your opponents are rushing 10 men. Executing this punt under such conditions is equivalent to hitting a grand slam in baseball; it will not happen often and should not be expected.

Don't concern yourself with any expectations for this situation except punting for distance. Regardless of any criticism you may incur from your coaches for lack of height on the punt, it is far more damaging to the strategic field position balance of the game to punt a short, high punt in this situation than to punt a lower, driving punt with good distance.

Besides, the punt team usually has some of the fastest and best-tackling players on the front line. They simply must be coached to give greater effort by running harder and covering farther on a punt that must be driven down the field for distance. There are two coaching options for this field punting situation: Coach the punt coverage team on how to cover a drive punt in this situation or coach the defensive team on how to play defense when deep inside their own territory. As a coach myself, I opt for coaching the punt coverage team.

Coffin-Corner Punts

A coffin-corner punt is directed toward the sideline with the intent of having the punt either go out of bounds or come to rest between the opponents' 20-yard line and their goal line. This punt is used when the football is positioned between the 50-yard line and the +30-yard line. In this field position, the opponents will generally line up to defend a possible fake punt, so there will be minimal rush. Thus, you will have no excuse for not punting the football in the proper direction to force your opponent to start their offensive possession as deep as possible in their own territory.

You can make no greater contribution to the success of your team and, in particular, the effectiveness of the defense, than to be a good coffin-corner punter. You can truly control your opponents' offense and decrease their chances of scoring by being able to execute the coffin-corner punt effectively. The team that can maintain the field position advantage will generally win the football game. Your role is to create and take the field position advantage for your team. Coffin-corner punting is the means for you to do this.

Coffin-corner punting is more effective than pooch punting (punting the football as high as possible straight down the middle of the field), because it eliminates the possibility of a return when you mishit the punt. The coffin-corner punt is directed away from the return man, who is coached not to field the football because he is in such a dangerous field position to make a fielding mistake.

In essence, if you become adept at coffin-corner punting, you will have an uncontested opportunity to execute this skill and take control of the field position advantage for your team. As with the hang-time punt, you will have no excuse for not executing the coffin-corner punt. If you cannot, it will be for the same reasons mentioned earlier, and once again, the coach should find a new punter.

THE PUNTER AND THE PUNT TEAM

Most coaches discourage a punter from using the three-step approach because they believe it requires him to cover more ground than a two-step approach. Although this can be true, it is false to assume more distance is covered because more steps are taken. It is the *length of the steps* that determines the distance a punter covers, not the *number of steps* he takes.

A two-step punter can cover just as much ground as a three-step punter if his steps are lengthened and the three-step punter's are shortened. Therefore, if you monitor the *distance* the punter covers with his steps, you do not have to worry about how many approach steps he is taking. A punter will naturally adapt the length of his steps without any coaching if he is given a specific distance to stay within as he punts. The recommended approach distance for a punter is four yards.

A four-yard approach allows the punter to stay behind the point that punt rushers normally run toward to block the punt. Punt rushers are coached to run to a point 9.5 yards behind the center snap to block the punt, because this is where most punters contact the football with their foot. Thus, if the punter stands 14 yards behind the center to receive the snap and covers a distance of four yards to punt the football, he will contact the football at 10 yards behind the center snap point, or a half yard behind where the punt rushers are heading to block the punt.

Consequently, if the punter stays within the four-yard approach distance, it doesn't matter whether he takes two or three steps to punt the football. Under these circumstances, he can take the number of steps that are natural for him. Putting an athlete in a setting that feels natural and comfortable will help him perform better.

If a punter is coached to stay within the four-yard approach distance as opposed to taking two or three steps, the coach can rest assured that the punter's approach steps are not contributing to getting the punt blocked and can focus on other details of coaching the punt team, for example, punt protection.

Coordinating the Punter's Release Time and Punt Team Protection

The punter has an obligation to punt the football within the amount of time that corresponds to the punt team's ability to protect him while he punts. The punt team has the responsibility to protect the punter long enough for him to perform to his maximum potential. The more the punt protection team can create this comfort zone for the punter, the better he can punt and the easier the punt team's job of covering the punt will be, because the punter will punt the football higher and farther.

For years, coaches have used a time of 2.1 seconds from the center snap to ball contact as a barometer of how quickly the punter must punt the football to avoid having it blocked. This time assumes that the punt protection team can only protect for 2.1 seconds or less and still cover the punt. It also forces the punter to quicken his approach to remain within the allotted time, even if taking a tenth of a second longer will maximize his ability.

Consequently, a coach can have a good punter who gets his best punts off in 2.2 to 2.3 seconds, but because he must rush his approach and mechanics, he does not punt the football as well as he is capable of. The coach now has exactly what he coached for—a punt release time of 2.1 seconds or less so that the punt will not get blocked. However, he also has a punter who is not performing at full potential.

The punt protection team *can* protect the punter longer than 2.1 seconds. This time should be viewed as an *average* time to punt the football, not a *standard* time. To determine the release time for the punter, the coach should chart the time it takes him to get off his best punts without rushing his approach.

In some instances, the extra release time for the punter can mean the difference in 0.3 to 0.5 seconds of hang time and five yards of distance on the punt. If this is the case, the punt team coach should spend more time coaching the punt protection personnel to protect longer so that the punter can get off better punts, making the punt team's coverage responsibilities easier. In any case, the punt protection should not dictate to the punter what his release time should be. The release time the punter needs to produce maximal punts, not to exceed 2.3 seconds, should determine the protection time.

Determining the Quickness of the Punter's Release Time

The factor that determines how quickly the punter punts the football is *not the number of steps* he takes but *how quickly* he takes those steps. Often a coach will insist that a punter take two steps to punt the football because he believes it is quicker and covers less distance than taking three steps, even if taking two steps significantly affects the punter's ability to punt well.

The formula for speed or quickness is distance multiplied by time. To increase speed or quickness, you decrease either the distance covered or the amount of time it takes to cover that distance. For a punter to decrease, or quicken, his release time, if the distance of his approach steps remains constant at four yards, he simply needs to step faster during his approach. However, he must be trained to quicken his steps without rushing the other mechanics, or he will not punt the football as well as he is capable of.

Finally, the coach should determine what release time, within 2.3 seconds, the punter performs best in and coach the punt protection for that speed. If the timing of the punter and punt coverage team are coordinated, the coach will have a punting unit performing at maximum efficiency and contributing to winning football games.

Coaching a Straight Approach Path for Punt Protection

A successful training method that can be used to teach the punter what a straight approach path feels like is to have him punt down a line (see drill 11). The line serves as a sightline to assist in keeping the position of the ball drop, the leg swing path, and the stepping approach path aligned in a straight line.

The line also provides the punter with instant feedback on his stepping approach path. After he finishes the punt, he can look down and see if his feet are on or off the line. If he finishes to the right or left of the line, he will know that he did not take a straight stepping approach path.

If the punter is practicing without a center to snap him the football and is having trouble keeping his approach path straight, the coach can position a cone behind him when he is in his stance and another one 10 yards directly in front of him. The cone in front will serve as a landmark to point the football at to set the punter on a straight track for his stepping approach.

The punter should also check his alignment with the front cone after he has contacted the football and completed the punt. If he finishes to the left or right of the cone, he will know he did not keep his stepping approach path straight. In either case, the front cone gives him a quick and easy way to discern which direction his stepping approach path took.

It is important for the punter to remain in the middle of the punt protection. In most punt-protection schemes, the punt protectors are fan blocking the rushers to the outside as the punter steps straight ahead to punt the football. Therefore, the punter must take a straight approach path for his protection to be successful. Veering to the left or right to punt the football shortens the distance the rushers from the outside have to run to block the punt.

There are only two situations in which it is okay for a punter to step to the right or left: when he is directional punting or coffin-corner punting. If a coach has elected to punt away from the punt returner (directional punt), the punter must walk to the left or right to punt the football. In this case, the coach will generally make the necessary adjustments in punt protection to match the punter's left or right approach path. To perform a coffin-corner punt, the punter also must walk to the right or left, depending on which corner of the field he is punting to.

In either of these situations, however, even though the punter is stepping to the right or left on his approach, he must still maintain a straight path. Whether it is a directional punt or coffin-corner punt, he will simply have a different landmark to point the football at and walk toward. Although it appears he is stepping to his right or left to punt the football, he is actually walking in a straight line, but the straight line is not straight down the field.

A straight stepping approach path allows the punter to learn only one approach method and apply it to different situations. Whenever an athlete can apply the same techniques in different situations, he has increased his opportunity for success.

Table 5.1 helps you coach yourself when you have punted a bad punt. Knowing what you did wrong and correcting it *before* the next punt will help you learn to apply the same techniques from punt to punt. This will make you a more consistent punter, helping you become the situation punter you need to be to help your team win.

Table 5.1

ASK THE COACH	
What's wrong with my punt?	**How do I correct it?**
The ball spirals to the left.	Move your drop arm out so the drop arm elbow is over the hip and walk straight down the field. *Practice drills:* Ball Drop and Down the Line Drills
The ball spirals to the right.	Move your drop arm in so the drop arm elbow is over the hip and walk straight down the field. *Practice drills:* Ball Drop and Down the Line Drills
The ball travels straight but end over end.	• Keep your shoulders in athletic position throughout the motion. • Walk straight down the field. • Straighten the nose of the football to point down the field. *Practice drills:* Leg Swing and Down the Line Drills
The ball goes left and end over end	• Straighten the nose of the football. • Move your drop arm out. • Swing straight. *Practice drills:* Leg Swing, Cone to the Right, and Down the Line Drills
The ball flies straight with nose up but doesn't turn over.	Make sure your wrist is straight, not pointing upward or inward. *Practice drills:* Ball Drop Drill

Table 5.1 *(continued)*

ASK THE COACH	
What's wrong with my punt?	**How do I correct it?**
The ball stays nose up but travels left.	• Keep your wrist straight in hand-shaking position. • Move the ball out over your hip. *Practice drills:* Ball Drop and Cone to the Right Drills
The ball stays nose up but travels right.	• Keep your wrist straight in hand-shaking position. • Move the ball in over your hip. *Practice drills:* Ball Drop Drill
The ball is a wobbly spiral traveling to the right.	• Keep your shoulders in athletic position. • Move the ball in over your hip. • Reposition elbow so it points at ground. *Practice drills:* Down the Line, Ball Drop, and Leg Swing Drills
The ball goes high but not far.	Remember to not drop the ball from chest height, but guide the ball down the drop line. *Practice drills:* Ball Drop and Through the Goalpost Drills
The ball goes far but not high.	• Keep the football at the starting drop height during approach steps. • Release the football smoothly and softly. • Do not push the football down or drop it too fast. *Practice drills:* Ball Drop and Hang-Time Drills

chapter 6

PRACTICE DRILLS FOR PUNTERS

Similar to kicking drill work, variety is *not* the spice of life for punting development. Select a few punting drills to develop the essential skills needed to become a good punter and master them.

There are more drills for punting in this chapter than there were for kicking in chapter 3. This is because the punter has one additional technique he must perform that the kicker does not—dropping the football. In addition, the punt flight objective sometimes emphasizes height over distance, distance over height, or direction over height and distance.

These are all different punt techniques you must practice in order to learn and execute. This is different than the ball flight purpose for a kicker. He has only one ball flight objective—high enough not to be blocked, far enough to get over the crossbar, and straight enough to go between the goalposts. This never changes for an extra point or field goal.

Remember as you do the drills, *quality* and *execution*, not quantity and repetition, must be practiced. Your leg is a muscle that can only perform so many repetitions before fatigue limits your drill training. Therefore, you should expect to concentrate from the very first punt to the last punt. Do not make excuses for yourself if the first punts are not as expected by saying, "It takes me awhile to get warmed up."

When you take the field to punt in a game, you only get one chance to succeed. Warm-ups are done on the sideline. So, warm up prior to doing the drills and do the drills for concentrating, executing, and performing to make yourself a good punter.

10 PARTNER BALL TOSS DRILL

Purpose:

This drill develops your catching and handling skills. It is good for improving your catching skills and release time by decreasing ball-handling time.

Procedure:

1. Stand 10 yards apart from your partner in a good punting stance.
2. Using one football, toss the ball underhand to each other, simulating a snap.
3. Each punter should catch the football, rotate the laces so they face upward, and raise the football into the drop position as quickly as possible.

Key Points:

Do this drill in two sets of 20 repetitions.

Text Review

The Snap and Positioning of the Football, pp. 73-76; *Vertical Ball-Drop Position for the Punt*, pp. 76-83.

DOWN THE LINE DRILL

Purpose:

This drill is a method for checking your straightness of form and body mechanics.

Procedure:

1. Stand on one of the lines on the football field or any straight line.
2. Punt the football using your normal steps, techniques, and punting rhythm.
3. When you finish the punt, you or your coach should check your finishing technique and the ball's flight before you move.

Key Points:

First, when you finish your leg swing, you should be standing directly on top of the line. If not, you are walking either left or right, depending on which side of the line you finish on. The other technique error you may be committing is swinging across your body to punt the football. Second, the flight of the football should cause it to land farther downfield but on the line or within a yard either side of it. If it does not land in this area, your leg swing was not straight through the football or the ball drop was turned too far inward. Check for the proper hand-shaking position of the football. Do this drill for 10 punts at least twice a week to check your straightness of form or when the football is not flying straight downfield consistently.

Text Review:

Approach Steps, pp. 93-100; *Approach Steps Technique Checklist*, p. 100.

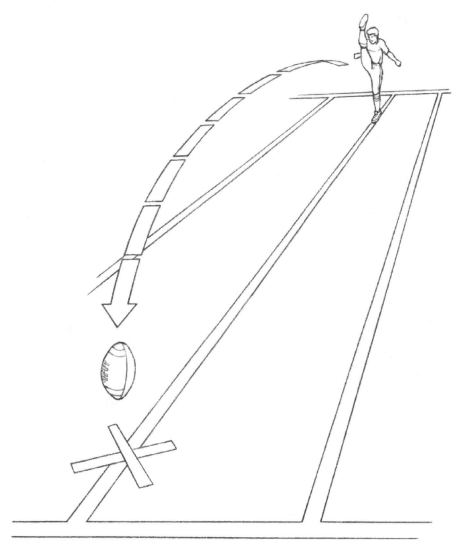

BALL DROP DRILL

Purpose:

Dropping the ball properly is one of the most important components of punting. This drill works on putting the football in the proper position to punt it. If you cannot put the football in a good hitting position consistently, it will be hard to be a successful punter.

Procedure:

1. Stand with your punting foot pointing straight down the line. Your hips, shoulders, and knees should also be pointing straight ahead.

2. Using the proper drop mechanics explained in the text, drop the football directly on the line. The ball should land flat and bounce straight back up toward you, not forward or backward.

Key Points:

Two sets of 25 drops should be done daily. Doing any more than 25 drops in one set will cause you to lose your concentration and result in lower-quality repetitions.

Text Review:

Vertical Ball-Drop Position for the Punt, pp. 76-83; *Vertical Ball-Drop Technique Checklist*, p. 83.

Purpose:

This drill teaches the two-step and three-step approaches. It will keep you from covering too much ground with your steps.

Procedure:

1. One towel is placed behind your heels after you have assumed your stance.
2. The other is placed four yards in front of you. You must take your steps and contact or punt the football behind or directly above the towel at the four-yard mark.

Key Points:

This drill is extremely effective in training you to contact the football behind the block point and in teaching the proper two-step and three-step approaches. It should be done twice a week in the pre-season and as needed during the season. Do not place too much emphasis on the approach steps, because they have little impact on the height and distance of the punt. Your only concern should be the number of yards you cover when punting the football.

Text Review:

Approach Steps, pp. 93-100; *Approach Steps Technique Checklist*, p. 100.

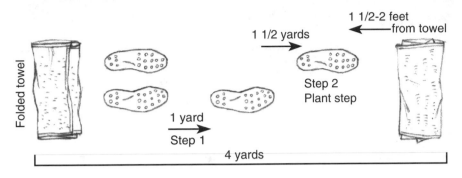

Folded towel

1 yard
Step 1

1 1/2 yards

1 1/2-2 feet
from towel

Step 2
Plant step

4 yards

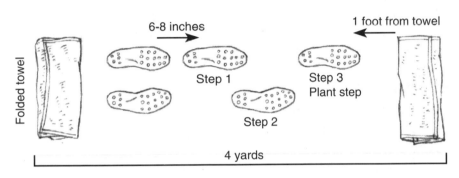

Folded towel

6-8 inches

Step 1

1 foot from towel

Step 3
Plant step

Step 2

4 yards

PARTNER CATCH DRILL

Purpose:

This drill is designed to assist you in making good, flat contact between your foot and the football. It also develops your ability to control the direction of the football, which is essential in coffin-corner punting.

Procedure:

1. Stand 35 to 40 yards across the field from a punting partner or coach.
2. Punt the football as if it were a pass directly to your partner. To do this, take one step with your plant leg, drop the football, and punt it to your partner.

Key Points:

You must keep the football flat, snap your leg quickly through the football, and push or propel it directly to your partner. For this punt to work, you must point your toe maximally at your partner and quickly snap your leg through the football. Do not punt the football for height or distance. Punt it accurately so your partner does not have to move.

Text Review:

The Ball Drop, pp. 83-92; *Ball-Drop Technique Checklist*, p. 92.

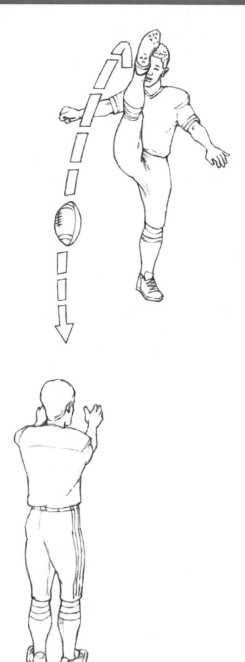

15 HANG-TIME DRILL

Purpose:

This drill is designed to train you to punt for height.

Procedure:

1. Choose a tall object—telephone pole, telephone wire, or tree—about 100 feet tall.
2. Stand 20 yards from the object. Using normal punting techniques, punt the football over the object or so that it travels as high as the object.

Key Points:

The only adjustment you need to make to punt a football this high and quickly is to hold the ball longer before punting it so that you can make contact with it higher off the ground. Do this drill once every two to three weeks for two sets of 10 repetitions.

Text Review:

Contact Height for Hang Time, p. 107; *Hang-Time Punts*, p. 122.

Purpose:

This drill is good for correcting punters who get good height on the ball but not enough distance. It works on the drive punt. It also assists in developing control of the football's direction of flight, which is essential for coffin-corner punts.

Procedure:

1. Stand at the 50-yard line facing one set of goalposts.
2. Using proper mechanics, try to punt the football through the uprights.

Key Points:

To do this drill successfully, you are forced to push the football down the field horizontally with your plant foot to get it through the goalposts. Do this drill every two to three weeks for two sets of 10 repetitions.

Text Review:

Contact Height for Distance, pp. 107-109; *Drive Punts*, pp. 122-123.

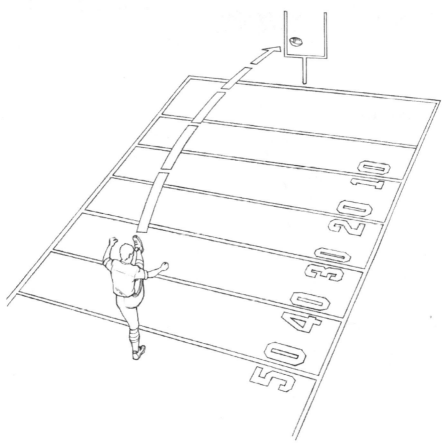

OUT OF THE END ZONE DRILL

Purpose:

This drill is designed to prepare you for the most dangerous situation you will face as a punter, so that when it occurs, you will feel comfortable and confident that you can perform.

Procedure:

1. Stand with your feet three inches from the back line of the end zone.

2. Using the two-step approach, catch and punt the football as quickly as possible.

Key Points:

Your coach should have someone watch your feet to be sure you do not step on the back line. If you do, it is a safety. Practice this situation at least once a week for 5 to 10 punts.

Text Review:

Two-Step Approach, pp. 94-96.

Purpose:

This drill teaches and trains correct leg swing form.

Procedure:

1. Using a straight line, position yourself the same as for the Ball Drop Drill, with your body pointing straight down the field and your punting leg on the line.

2. To do the drill, take a step with your nonpunting leg and then swing your leg, mimicking the punting motion straight down the line.

3. Choose a point six feet in front of where you are standing to focus your eyes on, and swing through this spot.

Key Points:

Two sets of 10 swings should be done for warming up prior to punting or three sets of 10 to train your leg to swing straight.

Text Review:

Leg Swing, pp. 109-113; *Leg Swing Technique Checklist*, p. 113.

6 feet

Purpose:

This drill is used to help correct a tendency to swing your leg across your body instead of in a straight line.

Procedure:

1. Place one cone 40 yards straight downfield from where you are punting and another 10 yards to the right of it.
2. As you punt the football, think about swinging your leg toward the cone on the right after contact with the ball.

Key Points:

If you swing toward the cone to your right your leg will be straight, even though you will feel like your leg is too far to the right. This is a natural progression of what it "feels" like to swing straight. Once you recognize what the correct swing feels like, it will become comfortable for you to swing straight after contact each time.

It should also feel as though you are not following through as much as before. This is because your thigh is now swinging straight through the football and hitting your chest instead of your left shoulder. Incorporate this drill into your normal punting workout to correct the crossover leg swing.

Text Review:

Punt Finish, pp. 113-116; *Punt Finish Technique Checklist*, p. 116.

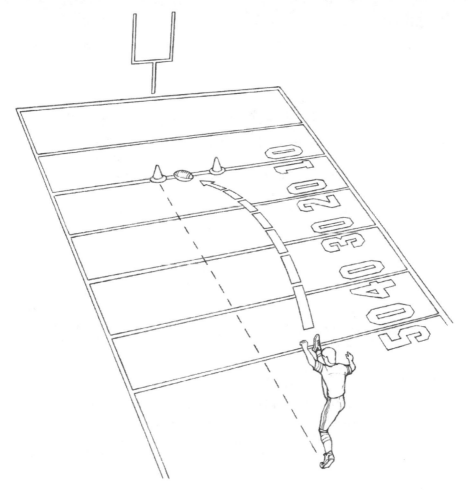

Purpose:

This drill is used to work on your ability to punt the football according to the field situation. It gives you great field perspective and trains you to know what type of punt is best for each field situation. Doing this drill is much more realistic than standing in one spot all the time and punting the same type of punt over and over.

Procedure:

1. Place two footballs on the 10-, 20-, 30-, 40-, and 50-yard lines.
2. Stand 10 yards behind the footballs and have someone snap them to you. If you do not have a snapper, move each set of footballs back 10 yards to the goal line, 10-, 20-, 30-, and 40-yard lines to do the drill.
3. Punt both footballs at a station and then move up the field to the next station.
4. Punt the appropriate type of punt—field punt, hang-time punt, drive punt, or coffin-corner punt—for where the ball is located on the field.

Key Points:

The footballs on the 10- and 20-yard lines require a drive punt or a punt that has more distance than hang time. The punts on the 30-yard line should have a good complement of hang time and distance (field punts). The punts from the 40- and 50-yard lines should have more hang time than distance (hang-time punts), but enough distance to be placed inside the 20-yard line. This drill should be done twice a week for two sets.

Text Review:

Situation Punting Field Positions, pp. 120-124.

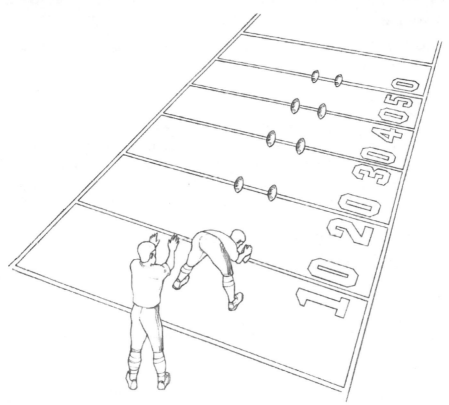

APPROACH STEP DRILL

Purpose:

This drill develops rhythm and smoothness in stepping and approaching the football.

Procedure:

1. Assume the proper stance as explained in the text.
2. Have someone toss you a football to simulate a snap, or you can throw the football and bounce it off the ground to yourself.
3. Once you receive the football, take steps and swing without punting the football. The football will drop to the side of your swing.
4. Practice both the two-step and three-step methods using this drill. Each method will be used in game situations.

Key Points:

One set of five repetitions of each stepping method is recommended for warm-up and two sets of 15 of each method for training.

Text Review:

The Punter's Stance, pp. 70-73; *Approach Steps*, pp. 93-100; *Approach Steps Technique Checklist*, p. 100.

Purpose:

This drill makes you keep the football in front of you and always field the snap. Do not allow yourself to not field a bad snap and say, "That one is just too bad. I'll never have to field one like that." It may happen in a game. This drill is similar to the Partner Catch Drill. The only difference is that the punter never receives a good snap.

Procedure:

1. Have someone throw you simulated snaps that are short, to the right, to the left, high, over your head, on the ground, at your feet, end over end, and so on.

2. Field the football and put it in the drop position as if you were going to start your approach steps to punt it.

Key Points:

This drill should be done twice a week for one set of 20 punts. Once you have trained yourself to field the snaps, you can begin fielding the snaps and then punting the football. You only need to do this drill with actual punting once every two to three weeks for 10 punts.

Text Review:

The Snap and Positioning of the Football, pp. 73-76; *Receiving the Center Snap Technique Checklist*, p. 75-76.

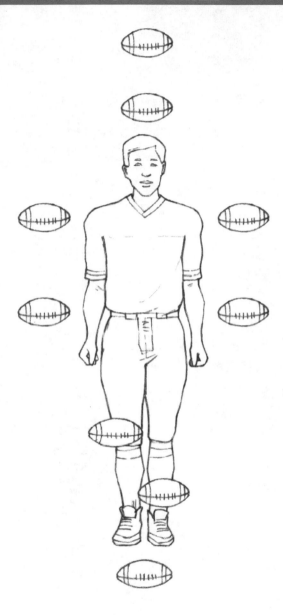

chapter 7

TRAINING AND CONDITIONING FOR KICKERS AND PUNTERS

t is important to establish proper and safe conditions in which to develop your punting and kicking skills. This consists of training and conditioning your body to be able to perform injury-free and with maximum muscular production. The three areas of training and conditioning you will use are strength training, speed or running training, and actual punting and kicking of the football.

How these three training and conditioning areas are scheduled and coordinated in a weekly and yearly training program will determine whether you get *something* out of it or get the *most* out of it. Getting the most out of training and conditioning is the goal of an athlete who wants to develop his abilities to maximum potential and master the skill. Getting something out of the training and conditioning is the goal of an athlete who only wants to perform well for the situation and will never learn the skill well enough to be able to perform on command. You must choose which philosophy you will subscribe and aspire to. Even if your decision is not a conscious one, your actions and effort as you perform your training and conditioning workout will tell everyone which philosophy you subscribe to.

Knowing and executing the proper technique of a skill is essential to performing the skill. Being able to perform the skill *better* than someone else is a direct result of your training and conditioning level.

An athlete with inferior or less well developed skills can compete with and beat an athlete with superior skills if he is better trained and conditioned to perform the skill at maximum level repeatedly. Sports is the greatest demonstrator that desire, motivation, and training and conditioning can overcome a deficiency in skill level.

Understanding the techniques of the skills of punting and kicking presented in this book will give you the knowledge you need to perform those skills effectively. However, it is what you do with that knowledge that is important. Your training and conditioning program is what you will use to develop your new knowledge.

DEVELOPING ATHLETIC ABILITY

It is a proven premise that better athletes learn athletic skills more quickly and can perform those skills better in competitive situations if they have been trained and conditioned properly. The purpose of the training and conditioning program is to develop athletic ability to assist you in performance of the skill. Although sport-specific training must be incorporated into the training program to develop those skills, the specific goal of training and conditioning is to make you a better athlete. Then, when an unusual situation arises—a bad snap on a punt, a mishandled snap on a field goal, having to punt on the run, having to kick from one step—an *athletic* punter and kicker will be able to perform and make the play to help his team win.

In teaching, training, and coaching punters and kickers, I have found that the best punters and kickers are also some of the best athletes. For purposes of this discussion, an athlete is defined as someone with good body coordination and balance, good eye-hand and eye-foot coordination, good agility, good running speed, good strength, good mental concentration, and the desire to be competitive and succeed. A good athlete does not necessarily possess exceptional qualities in any of these areas but is good in all of them.

You should not perform drills and train solely to be a good punter and kicker. Just punting and kicking the football will not develop all the physical and mental skills you need to reach beyond your maximum potential to become a top performer. The emphasis of your training and conditioning program, then, should be on making you a better athlete, which will in turn make you punt and kick better. Punters and kickers who do not train to be good athletes are just people who can punt and kick a football. Athletic punters and kickers are elite-level performers who can help their team win.

ESTABLISHING A TRAINING REGIME

To maximize your physical potential, you must have a training regime. The training regime is the vehicle you use to be able to perform a skill correctly multiple times. Performing multiple repetitions correctly is the only way you can become proficient at a skill. Without a training regime, you are depending on luck or chance for your success, which is the surest way to become an ex-athlete. A proper training regime has several components: a specific goal, a consistent plan or schedule, and sport-specific exercises. These three interrelated elements work together to comprise a proper training regime for the developing punter and kicker.

Each training component must have a specific goal or objective for improving your performance of the skill, in this case, punting and kicking. Whether you are weightlifting, running, or punting and kicking, you must know how the goal of each component of your training regime relates to your development as a punter and kicker. The goal is the purpose for doing the training. It will keep you focused on why you must do the training. Periodic adjustment of the goals is necessary as you accomplish existing goals. A training program without goals is like a boat without a rudder. It will drift aimlessly on the water. Eventually it may reach its goal of land, but only by chance. A punter or kicker whose training regime has no goals or objectives may reach his maximum potential, but it will only be by chance.

Once you have established your goals and objectives, you must develop a plan or schedule to help you achieve them. The goals will keep the plan focused, but the plan will develop your skills. The plan must detail *what* you should do, *how* you should do it, and *why* you should do it. If the plan omits any of these important details, it won't amount to much more than guesswork. It is possible to plan for success and *make* it happen!

Regardless of the goals you set, the single most important factor in determining whether you reach them is the consistency with which you do your training regime. You must make a commitment to be diligent in performing all the workouts in your training plan. Missing workouts, deciding not to do all of the scheduled exercises, or changing the plan in any way will keep you from reaching your full potential. The plan or schedule is pointless without your dedication and commitment to perform all the workouts and exercises. A simple saying to underscore this is to "plan the plan, and fly the plan." Those who "fly the plan" will be successful.

Sport-specific exercises are the mark of a good training regime. Whereas your training regime must have elements that will make you stronger, faster, and better athletically, the sport-specific exercises are what will translate these physical improvements into better punting and kicking performances. There are sport-specific exercises in the areas of strength, flexibility, speed, and plyometrics that will develop the primary muscles involved in punting and kicking. In addition, punting and kicking technique drills must be part of your daily training regime. These drills will develop you in the physical, mental, and technical aspects of punting and kicking. Any training program that makes you stronger, quicker, more flexible, and better athletically will benefit you, but sport-specific exercises will benefit you the most.

Drill Work

Every skill has specific mechanics that must be performed to execute that skill successfully. Drills are specific segments of a skill that you work on separately to make the entire skill better. The essential mechanics are the ones that should be practiced as drills so you can better execute the total skill. Repetitive drill work is the only method you can use to become a better kicker or punter.

You will progress through developmental stages as you do the drill work. Initially, your drill work will be used to develop technique consistency for the kick. You should notice yourself performing better on the drills after you have done them consistently for a few weeks. The drill work will give you confidence in your ability. Between your improvement in technique and your newfound confidence, you will begin to learn how to have command of the flight of the football. This can only be learned by doing segmented drill work, not by just kicking at goalposts.

Drill work should be done year-round with varying emphasis, depending on the time of the year. During the season, do drill work in areas where you are experiencing problems or for maintaining your technique. In the off-season, place your drill work emphasis on perfecting specific segments of the kick and allocate each segment a particular amount of instructional time for improvement. This is also the time when drill work must be the core of your training. Minimal time should be spent on actual performance kicking or kicking at goalposts because it will not improve your technique.

Drill work is done prior to special team work during the season. This helps prepare you for the team kicking period. Take a 10- to 15-minute rest prior to this time to allow for adequate recovery from the drills for better performance. Knowing how much drill work and how many kicks to do during this period is important. This is detailed for each kicking drill presented.

At times, drill work can seem tedious and unimportant. However, do not underestimate the importance of doing the drills. Far more time is spent training for a kick than actually performing it. You will not improve your kicking techniques during a game. That is when you must perform and not work on technique. Practice time is where you will improve. If done correctly, your practice drills must be more intense and more demanding than game situations.

Weight Training

Your year-round weight training program should be structured around the periodization method of training. This consists of an off-season, preseason, in-season and postseason training program that promotes continual muscular strength, power, and endurance gains. Performing each exercise with the correct technique is essential for proper transfer of your strength and power to punting and kicking the football. In addition, the intensity of training and the rest between workouts are significant contributors to your development.

The goal of your weight training program should be increasing your overall body strength with an emphasis on leg development. Stronger muscles will contract more forcefully, giving them the potential for greater power output. This power, applied with the proper punting and kicking techniques, will make the football go higher and farther. Strength training is a vital component of your development as a punter and kicker. If you neglect to develop the strength of your body, you will reach a plateau in terms of how high and far you can punt or kick the football. If you expect to reach an elite level of punting and kicking, you must strength train.

Your weight training program should include the following exercises: bench presses, incline bench presses, military presses, squats, leg extensions, leg curls, lat pulls, dips, arm curls, triceps extensions, and crunches. Other exercises that you like particularly well or that will complement these exercises can be incorporated into your program. Just remember that your goal is to develop your athletic ability, not to be a bodybuilder.

Running Training

The goal of the running program is to develop the aerobic and anaerobic capacities needed in a general conditioning program. It is a complement to the weightlifting and punting and kicking programs and is executed at 75 percent of maximum intensity. The running program has four phases: an endurance phase, a strength phase, a speed phase, and a maintenance phase.

Similar to the weight training periodization program, the running program cycles through a series of activities to reach peak muscular condition for the football season. It is important to remember that the running program is designed to help you punt and kick the football by training your legs properly to perform. Too much running or running with the wrong emphasis can inhibit your punting and kicking training.

The types of running you will perform within the four phases are endurance running, plyometrics, incline sprints, sprint/walk intervals, interval running, middle-distance runs, and sprints. Each type of running has a particular emphasis to promote the desired muscular benefit. A structured, sequenced program with developmental goals ensures maximum physical benefits and enables your body to respond to training better.

The running program is designed to assist in your leg speed development. It will increase your ability to achieve a faster leg speed when you swing at the football. This will increase the power you can impart to the football, causing it to travel higher and farther. As with the weightlifting program, the running program is a vital part of the training process for reaching your maximum physical potential. Failure to include or adhere to a comprehensive running program in your training will be detrimental to your performance as a punter and kicker.

Table 7.1 shows a year-round training plan for incorporating all three of these training elements to produce maximum results.* Some type of training in each of these elements year-round is essential for maximum physical development. Punting and kicking the football in and out of season is important for technique development, because they are fine motor skills that require precision of contact instead of brute force or power to be successful.

To properly train in all three areas you will often have to train in two areas on the same day. When you train in two areas on the same day, always do your punting and kicking drills first. Follow your drill work with running and end with weightlifting. On days where

Table 7.1

YEAR-ROUND TRAINING			
Month	Punting/Kicking	Running	Weightlifting
January	T, TH 25 punts/kicks	T Endurance	M, W, F Strength
February	T, TH 25 punts/kicks	T, TH Endurance	M, W, F Power
March	T, TH 25 punts/kicks	T, TH Endurance	M, W, F Power
April 1-15	T, TH 35 punts/kicks	T, TH Strength	M, W, F Adaptive
April–May	T, TH 35 punts/kicks	T, TH Strength	M, W, F Strength
June	T, TH 35 punts/kicks	T, TH Strength	M, W, F Power
July–August	M, W, F 35 punts/25 kicks	M, W, F Speed	T, TH Preseason program
August–November	M, T, W, TH, F Daily game week schedule	M, T, W (high school) M, T, W, TH (college) Daily in-season program	M, W In-season weight program
November–December	None	None	M, W, F

*For more details and information regarding the complete year-round training program for weightlifting, punting and kicking, and running, see Renner, B. 1993. *The Complete Manual to Punting and Kicking for Players and Coaches.* North Chelmsford, MA: Gridiron Press.

there is no planned kicking or punting, still run before weightlifting. Rest 20 minutes between punting/kicking and running, and 15 minutes between running and lifting. If you don't rest you risk injury. Also remember to thoroughly stretch before and between workouts.

INDEX

ABOUT THE AUTHOR

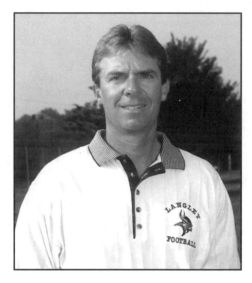

Bill Renner is a former NFL punter who played for the Green Bay Packers in 1986 and 1987 after a collegiate career at Virginia Tech.

Renner has directed punting and kicking camps since 1986 and has taught kickers throughout the United States since 1980. He has helped produce numerous all-district, all-state, all-region, and All-American performers.

Renner is a member of the American Football Coaches Association and the Virginia High School Coaches Association. He is currently head football coach and assistant athletic director at Langley High School (Virginia).

The author wrote his master's thesis on punting while earning an MS in exercise physiology from Virginia Tech University in 1983.

Renner and his wife, Cindy, have a daughter, Summer, and a son, Bryn. In his leisure time, Renner enjoys golf, skiing, and reading books.

Tom Taricani contributed his expertise to the soccer-style placekicking portion of the book. Tom is director of soccer-style kicking for the 4th Down Sports Kicking Camps. He has worked with the author for 10 years, developing and refining the teaching method that has proven so successful for hundreds of placekickers.

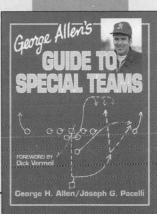
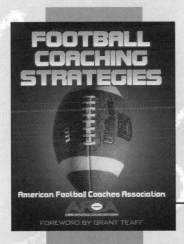

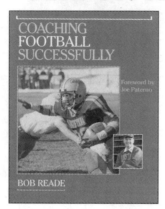
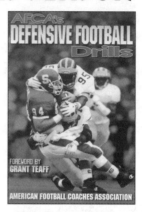